)f their own :
ıs

A League of Th

STEFFEN SIEBERT

★ ★ ★

A LEAGUE
OF THEIR OWN

THE SECRETS OF CLUB SOCCER CHAMPIONS

Meyer & Meyer Sport

British Library Cataloguing in Publication Data
A catalogue record for this book is available from the British Library

A League of Their Own
Maidenhead: Meyer & Meyer Sport (UK) Ltd., 2016
ISBN: 978-1-78255-105-8

© 2017 by Meyer & Meyer Sport (UK) Ltd.
Aachen, Auckland, Beirut, Cairo, Cape Town, Dubai, Hägendorf, Hong Kong,
Indianapolis, Manila, New Delhi, Singapore, Sydney, Tehran, Vienna

Member of the World Sport Publishers' Association (WSPA)

Total production by: Print Consult, Munich
ISBN: 978-1-78255-105-8
E-Mail: info@m-m-sports.com
www.m-m-sports.com

CONTENTS

INTRODUCTION

My starting point, like most coaches, was to simply work on getting the best out of my team. I asked myself one simple question: How can we get better every day? My goal was to always take one step forward, whether that was working to turn a poor team into an average team, transitioning a good team to a great team, or consistently keeping a great team at their peak (which is actually one of the most difficult endeavors in sport!). To do this, I decided that I needed to learn more about the certain approaches that coaches take and why, and how these approaches coincide with their principles and their vision. By exploring the patterns of how different coaches succeed more in-depth, I could better comprehend and formulate my own personal beliefs as a coach while incorporating different elements and applying them to my coaching style. I aimed to take the best of what the top coaches do, and integrate it into my own personal coaching philosophy.

This book will explore the history of some of the most famous soccer clubs in the world, and I will analyze the tactical setup of previous and current coaches. Additionally, this book takes a closer look at specific games, examining how the chosen teams set up to win the tactical battle and get the most out of each specific player. The teams that are focused on in this book are FIFA Club World Champions, such as Barcelona, who won this title in 2009, 2011, and 2015; Bayern Munich who won in 2013; and Real Madrid who won in 2014. Manchester City, a team that won the English Premier League in 2011-2012 and 2013-2014[1] is also included. The coaches of these clubs have also been named to highly prestigious awards.

---

1   See Wikipedia.

This book will explore the tactical setup and philosophy of coaching greats such as Pep Guardiola, who won FIFA Coach of the Year in 2011, and Luis Enrique who was named FIFA Coach of the Year in 2015[2]. The teams detailed in this book have key players that are known for their prowess at club level, as well as with their national team. These players include former national team captains such as Philipp Lahm (Germany), and current captains Robert Lewandowski (Poland), Cristiano Ronaldo (Portugal), and Lionel Messi (Argentina). The players at these clubs are perhaps the best in the world. There are no two names more well-known today in world soccer than Cristiano Ronaldo and Lionel Messi. These are the only two players who have taken home the Ballon D'Or in the past eight years—Messi has been awarded the trophy five times, and Ronaldo three times[3]. Finally, we will take an in-depth look at other special players who have been integral to their national teams that have won the two most recent FIFA World Cups (Spain in 2010, Germany 2014). It can be argued that these teams, their coaches, and the key players are among the best in the world. However, it still remains possible to beat these teams, and we can see more clearly how to do this when their tactical setup is broken down and analyzed.

In addition to the case studies of each team, I also provide a history of each club, and discuss the influence that recent coaches have had on these clubs. There will also be an in-depth discussion of the integral players for each club as well as how these players are used in the current and past systems. There will also be an in-depth discussion on the attacking and defensive setups under the current coach at these clubs.

A universal theme for every coach is that they have encountered a team that is more successful or talented than they. For this reason, I use case studies to analyze just how these great teams can be conquered, by whom, and how this was tactically achieved. I also provide a discussion of how the weaknesses of these great teams were exploited, thus defeated by teams despite their superior players.

One of the best aspects of soccer is that the use of proper tactical approaches and execution can make even the most superior team vulnerable to defeat. I aim to demonstrate how these great teams have been beaten. This involves a discussion of the adjustments that teams have made to defeat these top teams, as well as

---

2   *Ibid.*
3   *Ibid.*

to demonstrate the many options that exist to beat the great teams with the right tactical know-how. Winning the tactical battle on the soccer field creates endless possibilities, which is one of the most intriguing aspects of soccer.

HISTORY OF THE 4-2-3-1

The 4-2-3-1 system of play is perhaps the most widely used system in professional soccer over the last decade. This formation has been highly successful, likely due to its setup in midfield, using two defensive midfielders and three offensive midfield players.

Tactical formations in professional soccer have evolved over the years to match the increasing talent of the modern player. During the 1990s, the primary formation, used by the majority of the top teams in the world, was 4-4-2. It wasn't until the end of the 1990s[4] that the 4-4-2 formation began to evolve. Slowly, the midfield four that was seen in the 4-4-2 formation began to cool to a more flexible 4-2-3-1. In fact, France even used this formation before it was cool, winning the World Cup in 1998 and UEFA European Championship in 2000. Two other key teams that utilized the 4-2-3-1 was AC Milan under manager Arrigo Sacchi, and the Brazilian national team with Mario Zagallo.

More teams gradually began to understand the power of using this kind of midfield shape. To control the center of the field effectively using three players, as compared to the two traditionally used in the 4-4-2 shape, increased the chance of having a stranglehold on the game, thus increasing the likelihood of winning. Additionally, the 4-4-2 would have the wingers pushed more centrally; in the 4-2-3-1, these wingers now had the freedom to move more dynamically on the field.

As a result of these patterns many goals were created through zone 14 (see page 11), located in the middle of the field, immediately outside the 18-yard box.

---

4   See Wikipedia.

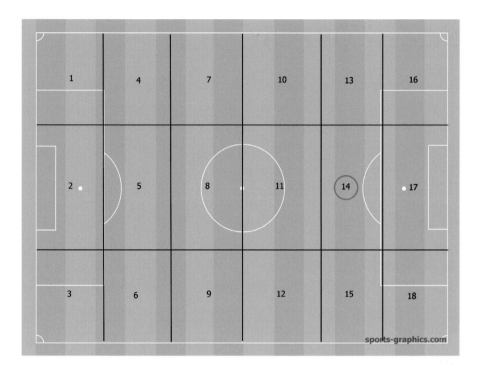

In order to combat against this defensively, teams placed two holding midfield players in this area (zone 14), attempting to cover the most technical players, who were trying to receive the ball.

SYSTEM OF PLAY

Choosing a system of play requires considerable effort and reflection for a coach. The coach must have a good grasp on his or her own philosophy and approach to coaching, and of course the game of soccer. The coach must ask himself: What is my coaching philosophy and vision? What types of players do I currently have and whom can I obtain? What are the approaches that are non-negotiable for me? What is the level of talent, and the tactical setup from the opposing team(s)? The answers to these questions will greatly shape how a coach aims to implement their vision into the tactical approach.

The four moments that remain constant during a match are attacking, transition to defense, defending, transition to attack, and back to attacking. Attacking and defending serve as the umbrella for these aspects and there are principles of play that remain constant for offense and defense.

DEFENDING

The primary focus of defending revolves around pressure, cover, balance, compactness, and control & restraint. I will discuss each of these at greater length.

1.   Pressure

When pressuring the ball, the players must learn to make a decision during the game as to where they will establish pressure. This decision will be shaped by the coach's overarching defensive philosophy, and the coach will train the player to recognize the triggers that call for different types of pressure.

The coach must first decide if he wants the player(s) to pressure high up the field, or to pressure a specific opposing player. Again, this will depend on their overall philosophy. Coaches with a high control approach, such as Guardiola or Enrique, will utilize an intense pressing system. The aim of this system is to win the ball back as soon as possession is lost. Therefore, they may train their players to push higher, which places greater pressure on the opposing ball carrier.

The decision of where and how the team will pressure the opposing player is influenced by the quality of players that the opponent has. The final question in determining the timing of pressure is: Where should the players ideally be placed to attempt to win the ball back? Teams that prefer to build up slowly from the back may be more comfortable winning the ball in their own third. Teams that tend to be more aggressive may look to win the ball back in their offensive third, attempting as a result to give themselves more scoring opportunities.

2.   Cover

The second area to focus on defensively is covering the player who puts pressure on the ball. These players provide support to the defender pressuring the ball. The decision here is whether to use man-marking, zonal defending, or even a mix of both. Another factor to consider regarding coverage is where and when the defender should track the opposing player, or if he should stay connected to the rest of the line. This is a scenario that will likely depend on the type of opponent that the team is playing against.

3.   Balance

The player(s) providing balance is responsible for assisting the defense in maintaining a good shape. They must be able to view the field and anticipate changes by the offense.

4.   Compactness

The final aspect of defending is compactness. Compactness refers to the degree of space between the players of a given team. The goal for defenders is to reduce the space between their own players to limit the ability of the attacking team to find space between the defending team.

The key is to be as compact horizontally and vertically as possible. A coach who utilizes a zonal style of defending will likely require less space between the players and between the lines (back-line, midfield players, forwards). The zonal-minded coach will look to eliminate space for the opposing team to receive the ball within their own formation, forcing them to use the outside channels instead.

Conversely, the coach who prefers to use man-marking or a mix of zonal and man-marking may allow for greater degrees of space. Both of these approaches have benefits and consequences. The overall coaching approach will help shape the degree of risk that a coach is willing to take. A coach who uses man-marking and intense pressure may be able to win the ball back quicker than a zonal approach, but at the same time they also risk leaving space between defenders, or even behind the defensive line.

Talented players such as Messi, Lewandowski, or Bale, who are known for their technical ability and speed, could possibly exploit this space. Therefore, we see just how important it is for a coach to develop a well-thought-out philosophy, as this will guide the coach in making well-informed tactical decisions to match his philosophy.

ATTACKING

The attacking side of the game tends to be less structured than defense. One explanation for this is that players are given the freedom to be creative. This is not to say that an attacking structure does not exist; however, it may not necessarily be as structured as the defensive side of the game and therefore leaves more room for creativity. One of the primary attributes of a good attack is how well the players can improvise and look to disrupt the organization of the defending team. The offensive players are constantly looking for ways to get past the defense. There are four primary motives that the offense is looking to attain, and these will be discussed further below.

1. Penetration

The term penetration means to force a way through, often by overcoming resistance. The coach who uses a more forceful style of attack may look to penetrate as quickly as possible even if that results in a high risk of losing the ball right away again.

A less forceful way of penetration would be to penetrate through the thirds of the fields by patiently passing horizontally until space opens up. Coaches may look to do this by attacking down the flanks, exploiting width to then cross the ball into the box, or through the use of combination. Again, this tends to also be influenced by the creativity of the individual player plus his technical ability, and tactical knowledge.

However, the coach must determine how he wants the team to start attacking. Is the goal to slowly build up the attack from the back? Is it to play the long ball with the aim of winning possession in the opposing final third? Or does the team look to use short passes to move the ball up the field? The coach often influences these strategies.

2. Support

The primary focus in the supporting aspect of attack is to determine where support is necessary, and how the team looks to possess the ball. The key aspect of support is the responsibility of the players who do not have possession. The coach may look to push the outside backs high up the field to stretch the opposing defense, or he may drop a midfield player deeper to help the back four build up from the back. The specific roles and responsibilities of each player in an attack will largely be determined by the specific strategy, as well as the overall approach.

3. Width

Contrary to a defensive approach, the attacking players will look to stretch the defense in the hope of creating more space to attack the goal. While the defense looks to maintain compactness, the offense looks to exploit width, perhaps by using their outside backs to push high up the field. This then forces the defenders to either leave gaps in their formation or leave players unmarked.

The location and timing of the width will be determined by the attacking strategy. Some coaches prefer to keep their outside backs deeper, and have their wingers provide the width, while others will allow outside backs to push up higher than the wingers to be able to overload certain areas. Other coaches may allow their outside backs to push higher when they build slowly from the back as opposed to if there is a quick counter attack.

4. Mobility

Mobility, similar to width, is used to break down the defense. The primary goal of mobility is to use movement of individual players to move the opposing players in specific areas to then exploit them. These movements can be difficult for a defender to anticipate, and frequent mobility, when executed correctly, can be effective in breaking down the defense.

In summary, the question that a coach must ask when determining a tactical approach is how rigidly he should keep to the system or formation. A key to successful coaching is recognizing when to make adjustments, yet it is important to recognize how these adjustments will fit into the overall philosophy.

WHY A 4-2-3-1?

There are specific reasons and benefits to using a 4-2-3-1 set-up. Perhaps one of the largest benefits is that this system incorporates four lines of players instead of the typical three as is seen in a 4-4-2 or 3-5-2. If there are four lines, they tend to have a higher degree of connectivity, making it more difficult to lose contact between them. This allows the offense to stretch the defense, creating more space and goal scoring opportunities for themselves.

Furthermore, it shortens the passing distances as compared to having three lines on offense. There are more options to choose from in the attack, and since the players are closer together, it becomes easier to quickly interchange positions, as seen in the Barcelona squad. This quick interchange makes it very difficult to defend, as the defense must anticipate these changes quickly. The back four in this setup are effective, especially when in possession as the full back can push higher up the field to provide support in attack, as well as to increase numbers in the attacking situation.

On the defensive side, there are also benefits to using a 4-2-3-1. Due to the compactness of the formation, there is a greater degree of flexibility, as the wingers only need to drop approximately 8-10 yards to create a 4-4-2 shape when defending. The 4-2-3-1 is a highly effective system because of the four lines of formation. This limits the running that the player must do, allowing them to play for longer at a higher intensity. These lines of four also create triangles or rectangles when defending, which can cut off passing lanes or dribbling opportunities for the other team.

There are many benefits to using the 4-2-3-1 with the main idea that having four lines instead of three can assist the players in adapting quickly to the opponent. It can also easily transition into several different formations such as a 4-1-4-1, 4-4-1-1, or 4-3-3 throughout the game. Finally, the use of three midfielders automatically provides more options defensively and offensively.

To avoid being caught unprepared, a coach must be aware of some potential limitations when using a 4-2-3-1. First, it is possible to become defensively isolated on the flanks. This may occur when playing against a team utilizing a 4-3-3 system or a 4-4-2 system. It is possible to be outnumbered by the other team when they are attacking from the flanks. Second, the coach must be aware that the team will need to manage the space that is created behind the full backs when the team is attacking. Perhaps the biggest limitation in using a 4-2-3-1 is the space created between the outside back and the winger. When the team is defending, they need to know how to manage these situations when they occur so as not to continually be exploited.

LEAGUES OF THE WORLD

LA LIGA (SPANISH)

The fact that the Spanish La Liga has traditionally been a two-horse race has not diminished its' popularity in world soccer circles. FC Barcelona and Real Madrid are arguably the two most recognizable teams in the world and certainly have the prestige and silverware to back up this claim. There is no doubt though that this league consists of more than these two giants of the game; Atletico de Madrid won the title in 2014[5], and teams such as Sevilla, Valencia, and Atletic Bilbao are widely respected across Europe.

The type of soccer played in La Liga can be characterized as an extremely technically advanced style. Even the teams toward the bottom end of the standings possess some very astute technicians. Due to the technically proficient style, the tempo of matches traditionally moves at a slower pace. The flow of the game also tends to be interrupted more in La Liga due to the increased number of stoppages for foul play.

ENGLISH PREMIER LEAGUE

The English Premier League has steadily grown in stature since the change to its current format before the 1992-1993[6] season. It is now widely considered to be the

---

5 *See Wikipedia.*

6 *Ibid.*

most entertaining league in the world due to the exciting brand of soccer it produces from all of its teams on a weekly basis.

While it may not be described as the most technically advanced league, the lure of the Premiership comes from the intense tempo at which each game is played. From the top of the table to the bottom, it is expected that a Premier League game will be played at a blistering pace from start to finish. In fact, the fans demand this type passion out of their players, more so than any other qualities, which is evident in the resulting style of play. The Premier League has seen a steady increase of technical players from abroad, and this has only enhanced its reputation. However, it is the more athletic players that truly thrive in this up-tempo environment.

The top teams in this league are household names, regardless of where you live in the world. Teams such as Manchester United, Arsenal, Liverpool, Manchester City, and Chelsea have large fan bases everywhere and their popularity often exceeds that of the local teams.

The financial amount distributed into the Premier League via television deals exceeds most other leagues and the Premier games are readily available throughout the world. There are large amounts of money available to these teams, even the lower standing teams. This allows the clubs to spend high amounts of money in search of the best players in the world, many of whom now make a living playing in England.

BUNDESLIGA (GERMAN)

The German Bundesliga has experienced somewhat of resurgence in recent years after temporarily falling a little off the map in the mid-2000s.[7] It has unquestionably overtaken Italy's Serie A and has become one of the top three leagues in Europe again, along with the Premier League and La Liga. One of the defining attributes of the Bundesliga is their dedication to the fans, creating a very fan-friendly league. In fact, it is said that Borussia Dortmund has the best fan atmosphere of any other club in the world. The majority of the stadiums are modern and accessible while the ticket pricing is reasonable compared to the other big leagues in the world. The fan experience is very special in this league, characterized by a deep passion for the

---

7 *Ibid.*

game. This passion is likely fueled by the history that soccer has in Germany; soccer was a key factor in uniting the divided Germany during the 1990s.[8]

Bayern Munich has dominated the league as of late and they possess the financial clout over their rivals. However, the league still possesses a plethora of great sides that play attractive soccer, including Borussia Dortmund, Wolfsburg, and Schalke 04.

COMPARISON BETWEEN LEAGUES

As one would expect, the three power leagues differ significantly in style and content. La Liga and Bundesliga have distinct dominating teams in Barcelona and Real Madrid, and Bayern Munich respectively. Bayern Munich have won six of the last ten Bundesliga titles and aside from the aberration of Atletico Madrid in 2014, Barcelona and Real Madrid have won every other La Liga title during the same period.[9]

The Premier League is perhaps better known for its unpredictability among all of the teams. While only three teams (Manchester City, Manchester United, and Chelsea) have won the title during the past 10 years[10], there are regular challenges from other teams in the league, such as Liverpool, Arsenal, and Tottenham Hotspur. In fact, the 2015-2016 season in England is particularly open as Leicester City, a team that was recently promoted from the English Championship League (2nd division) in 2014, top the table.

In terms of style, the tempo and aggression of the Premier League is renowned for being the highest. To the contrary, La Liga is considered to be methodical and technically advanced. The Bundesliga, on the other hand, is considered the middle ground between the Premier League and La Liga. One could also argue that the level of coaching is higher in the Bundesliga.

There is a reason that the best players in the world are attracted predominantly to these three leagues. All three of these leagues offer the most opportunity for European glory. However, the top players tend to be signed by the most financially powerful

8   *Ibid.*
9   *See Wikipedia.*
10   *Ibid.*

teams in the league, especially in Germany and Spain. The English Premier League, however, tends to have more financial distribution that allows for more clubs (even lower ranked clubs) to have the spending power to keep their top talent a little longer.

COMPARISON TO THE REST OF EUROPE

In terms of European competition, it is La Liga that is currently experiencing a wave of consistent success, creating a sizeable lead in the UEFA Coefficient country rankings, which are based on the results from the previous Champions and Europa League of the clubs from each European country.[11] In other words, La Liga teams tend to have the best performances in these tournaments, leading them to rack up more points for their league.

The last three Champions Leagues have now been won by Barca and Real, and Sevilla now won three straight Europa Leagues. It is evident that the Spanish sides are currently collecting the big prizes. However, success tends to run in cycles. During the mid- to late 2000s, the Premier League had a massive surge of success. In 2013, the Champions League final was a German affair between Bayern Munich and Borussia Dortmund. Even Italy's Serie A was highly successful in Europe with both AC Milan and Inter Milan having won the Champions League within the past ten years.

The current UEFA Club coefficient top 10 rankings consist of three Spanish teams, two German teams, two English teams, and one team each from Portugal, France, and Italy.[12]

The UEFA teams measure up enormously well to any other teams they face from around the globe. There are certainly specific reasons that the top players on the planet yearn to play in Europe. Each year, FIFA holds a World Club Championship tournament, which pits the winner from each confederation against each other in a small tournament. In the past ten years, a UEFA team has won the tournament eight times, showcasing their current soccer superiority.

---

11   *Ibid.*

12   *Ibid.*

FC BARCELONA

HISTORY

One of the most famous soccer clubs in the world, FC Barcelona was founded by Joan Gamper in 1899[13] due to the interest in soccer that spread from England. Gamper believed sport to be a way of boosting the human spirit and sought to instill the ideals of social integration and democracy into the club. The famous blue and claret uniforms have been a part of the club's history from the very beginning. An interesting fact about these historical colors is that they originated from FC Basel, Gamper's previous club before migrating to Barcelona. In 1910[14], Carles Comamala, a player at the time, created the current coat of arms for the team, a symbol that is now known around the world.

Barcelona's current stadium, The Nou Camp, was constructed in 1957, seats 99,345 people, and is the largest stadium in Europe. Barcelona possesses the bragging rights for the most La Liga titles and Copa del Rey championships, the oldest Spanish soccer competition. FC Barcelona has the largest fan base on social media compared to all other sport clubs globally. Other evidence of the superiority of this club includes the highest number of Ballon d'Or trophies awarded to players in history. The Ballon d'Or is the annual soccer award given to the best male player by FIFA, the sport's governing body. Barcelona's most prolific time was from 2004 to 2012 during which they won six league titles, two Copa del Rey's, five Supercopa de Espana titles, three

---

13   See Wikipedia.
14   Ibid.

UEFA Champions League titles, and two UEFA Super Cup Titles. In fact, since 1992, it has been a rare season that FC Barcelona did not win a title.

Team Motto: *Més que un club. ("More Than a Club.")*

HONORS

- ★ UEFA Champions League: 5
- ★ UEFA Cup Winner's Cup: 4
- ★ UEFA Super Cup: 5
- ★ FIFA Club World Cup: 3
- ★ La Liga: 23
- ★ Copa Del Rey: 27
- ★ Supercopa de Espana: 11

FC BARCELONA COACHES

JOSEP "PEP" GUARDIOLA (2008-2012)

The 45-year-old Spanish international spent the large majority of his playing career at Barcelona, where he made over 250 appearances for the team. During his time with Barcelona, the team secured an impressive seven league titles. He went on to play with various teams before his retirement in 2006. During his playing career, Pep made 47 appearances for the Spanish National Team and was a member of the team that took the gold medal at the 1992 Olympic Games.[15]

Pep Guardiola began his coaching career with the FC Barcelona "B" squad. After an enormously successful first season with this team, he was quickly promoted to head coach of FC Barcelona's first team. He enjoyed four years of sustained success between 2008 and 2012. In just his first season as coach for the main team, Pep led the squad to the Copa del Rey and La Liga championships in which they secured the title in both. He wrapped his first season up by taking home the UEFA Champions League

---

15   *See Wikipedia.*

to complete the treble. The following three years saw his team win a staggering ten additional honors both domestically and in Europe, including the 2010-2011 UEFA Champions League.

Guardiola's Barcelona team is seen by many as one of the most successful sides to have ever been assembled. This success was measured by the sheer number of trophies they won in combination with the dominating style of play. Guardiola's emphasis was to out-possess the opponent for extended periods of the game. At the beginning of his head coaching tenure with FC Barcelona, Pep focused on discovering players that fit this style of play and whose strengths were best emphasized by extended possession of the ball. If the player didn't fit in, he let them go despite the big names of certain players like Deco and Ronaldinho, both of whom were considered big stars at the time.

Under Guardiola, there was a clear system and strategy: positional play. In other words, when Barcelona was in possession of the ball, each player had to be positioned on specific parts of the field outlined in horizontal and vertical lines. Additionally, the players needed to be aware of their angles to each other and the opponent in order to create triangles and diamonds all over the field. Defensively speaking, Pep structured a highly intense pressing game that required all eleven players on the field to take part in this high pressing system the moment they lost possession.

The main difference between this particular FC Barcelona team (2008-2012) and others was not in the amount of top stars they had. Rather it was the degree of discipline that Pep instilled in each player. This was apparent when even top stars such as Messi and Iniesta were working incredibly hard defensively.

HONORS AT FC BARCELONA
★ La Liga Titles: 3
★ Copa del Rey: 2
★ UEFA Champions League Title: 2
★ UEFA Super Cup: 2
★ FIFA Club World Cup: 2

TITO VILANOVA (2012-2013)

Tito Vilanova, a Spanish native, spent his entire playing career (1988-2001) in Spain. The majority of his playing career was with UE Figueres, a club in the lower divisions. Although Vilanova was never able to make a name for himself as a player in the top division of the La Liga, this was not to be the case for his coaching career.

Vilanova's managerial career began with Palafrugell, which was followed by a big move to Barcelona as an assistant coach under Pep Guardiola. During this time, he experienced high degrees of success. In 2012, Vilanova stepped in to fill Guardiola's shoes as the head coach for Barcelona, soon leading them to a league title.

Comparing Guardiola's side with Vilanova's side, Tito did make several changes, but primarily continued with the strategy that led Barcelona to such great success. One of the primary changes was an increase in the dominating style of play. Vilanova accomplished this by pushing the outside backs higher on the flanks, even more so than Guardiola did. The likes of Dani Alves (right back) came close to melding into a right forward. Vilanova attempted to compensate for this aggressive style by dropping the defensive center midfielder (Sergio Busquets) deeper. This did pose somewhat of a problem for Barcelona as it blocked some of Busquets primary strengths, such as reading the game and forcing teams into certain pressure pockets or just outright winning the ball back.

Another change that Vilanova made was reducing the consistent pressing after Barcelona lost possession, a hallmark of the previous Barcelona squad. In regards to player personnel, Vilanova did not make major changes regarding the positions of certain main players when he took over. Overall, Vilanova kept the status quo established by Guardiola but made his mark on the squad as well.

Tragically, Vilanova was forced to retire following the 2012 season due to a cancer diagnosis. He passed away at the age of 45 on April 25, 2014.[16]

HONORS AT FC BARCELONA
★ La Liga Title: 1

---

16   See Wikipedia.

GERARDO MARTINO (2013-2014)

The 53-year-old Gerardo Martino spent the majority of his playing career at Newell's Old Boys, an Argentinian soccer club. Martino enjoyed three separate spells at the club, being a member of three league championship teams. Martino holds the record for most appearances for Newell's Old Boys.[17] However, the Argentinian was unable to make a name for himself as a national team player, making only one appearance for his country.

Martino's coaching career began in 1998 with Brown de Arrecifes, another Argentian soccer club, and he continued to bounce around clubs until he became the head coach for Paraguay (2006-2011). Martino then returned to his former club, Newell's Old Boys, for one season before being named as coach for FC Barcelona, a stint that lasted one season. Martino's most successful coaching position was with Club Libertad, a Paraguayan soccer club, where he won the league title on three occasions.

Martino's primary strategic approach, with its emphasis on attacking and pressing, was very fitting when he arrived at Barcelona. The two things that Martino stood for prior to his arrival at Barcelona were pressing and offensive play. Two of Barcelona's essential players, Xavi and Fabregas, were excellent fits for this style of play as Martino gave them permission to operate at their position with more freedom. This allowed Xavi and Fabregas to make better use of the attacking third. Before Martino's arrival, the Barcelona center midfield players were set up to play and move more horizontally across the field than vertically. The adjustments that Martino made allowed for Fabregas and Xavi to make more vertical, penetrating runs, and both became bigger scoring threats and assisting goals themselves.

Vilanova's defensive structure of high outside backs was no longer feasible as Barcelona struggled with maintaining defensive stability. Martino adjusted this by keeping the two outside backs deeper than previously and used the forward wing players to provide the width in the system. Despite making these subtle changes, Martino largely kept to the Barcelona philosophy of pressing and controlling through possession.

HONORS AT FC BARCELONA
★   Supercopa de Espana: 1

---

17   Ibid.

LUIS ENRIQUE (2014-PRESENT)

Luis Enrique is the 65th manager in 2008, and one of the rare few who also played for the team. In 2008 Enrique returned to the club as the coach for the "B" team, taking over from Guardiola who moved to the main squad. Interestingly enough, this was the same start for Pep Guardiola, first as a player, then as "B" coach, and finally as head coach of the main team. While at the reins of the 'B' team, Enrique was integral in bringing the team back to the Segunda Division in just his second season. He then moved on to AS Roma (2011-2013) and Celta de Vigo (2013-2014), but deep down, he always longed to return to the club that had been such a major part of his life.

Enrique was named as FC Barcelona's head coach in May 2014. Since this appointment, Enrique has won every major honor in soccer, again following in the footsteps of his former mentor, Pep Guardiola.

HONORS AT FC BARCELONA
* La Liga: 1
* Copa del Rey: 1
* UEFA Champions League: 1
* UEFA Super Cup: 1
* FIFA Club World Cup: 1

FC BARCELONA'S KEY PLAYERS

GERARD PIQUÉ (2008-PRESENT)

Despite growing up in the Barcelona youth system, Gerard Piqué made his professional debut with Manchester United. He returned to the Nou Camp from Old Trafford after a four-year spell[18] to rejoin his boyhood club and has not looked back.

The 29-year-old Spanish native is unquestionably one of the most graceful central defenders in world soccer. Although possessing the elite size of 6'4", he is by no means known for his physicality. Instead, it is Piqué's ability on the ball that has made him such a massive success for club and country. As Barcelona usually dominates possession of the ball, Piqué rarely sees consistent pressure from the opposition. Instead, he is the ideal man to initiate attacks from the back four and is the playmaker when the opposition defends deep.

Piqué tends to start the attack with the help of Busquets, who drops in next to him, or Rakitic, who will check back to collect the ball from him. Piqué has played the same position under all recent managers. The only tactical difference was seen under Pep and now Enrique, as the back four hold a higher line to stay connected with the rest of the team when counter pressing the opposition.

Piqué has won almost every major honor possible for a player. He has won both the Champions League and La Liga titles on multiple occasions. Piqué is one of only four players on Barcelona's squad to have won the UEFA Champions League title in two seasons. He has also won the European Championships and the World Cup with Spain, having made over 70 appearances for his country since his debut in 2009.

SERGIO BUSQUETS (2008-PRESENT)

The 27-year-old Sergio Busquets has been the anchor for the Barcelona squad since his debut in 2008. He has been an ever-present part of their starting eleven at the holding midfield position. In many ways, Busquets could be described as the perfect

---

18   *See Wikipedia.*

modern day holding midfielder. Although he stands at an impressive 6'2", it's the non-physical skills that make him such a master of his craft.

Busquets possesses incredible awareness and capability in closing off potential spaces where other teams might play. He regains the ball to then distribute back to his own team. While a typical holding midfielder may look for the 1-v-1 battles, Busquets focuses on winning the ball before these 1-v-1 situations arise by anticipating where the ball might go.

Busquets is a highly intelligent player and excels at anticipating where he needs to move offensively in order to create space to receive the ball. This could occur in the midfield line or by dropping between the two center backs. This creates the possibility for Barcelona to push their outside backs high, or to use Busquets's movement to draw a defender with him, opening up space for his team to receive or dribble the ball into.

He also possesses above average technical skills, allowing him to fit seamlessly into the offensive side of the Barcelona style as well. With these numerous specific skills, it is not surprising that he has consistently maintained his position throughout his career at Barcelona, even with varying coaches.

Busquets has won many of the major honors available; he has been a key member of Spain's victories at the World Cup in 2010 as well as the European Championships in 2012. Busquets has over 80 caps for the Spanish national team.[19] He has also won many prestigious titles at the Nou Camp with Barcelona.

ANDRÉS INIESTA (2002-PRESENT)

Andrés Iniesta is the current captain of the Barcelona squad, inheriting the armband in the 2015-2016 season after former captain, Xavi, left Barcelona. It is not an overstatement to label Iniesta as one of the top players of his generation. The man is basically incomparable when it comes to the honors he has achieved with Barcelona and the Spanish national team. The diminutive Spaniard is not physically imposing in the slightest, but has been a thorn in the side of every team he has faced since his debut from the Barcelona academy (2002) at the age of 18.

---

19   See Wikipedia.

It takes a special player to be a standout among the many brilliant Barcelona players, but Iniesta has proven to be a key man throughout his entire time at the Nou Camp. Although he has operated in a variety of positions under the last few coaches at Barcelona, Iniesta's primary position under former coach Pep Guardiola was as the left-sided center midfielder alongside Xavi. Pep made enormous use of Iniesta's unbelievable ability to keep possession of the ball under even the most immense pressure, a key component for Barcelona in the Pep Guardiola era.

Under Gerardo Martino, Iniesta primarily stayed as the left center midfielder, but used more vertical direction to get higher up the field. He was also used in the left forward role from time to time to capitalize on his ability to combine under pressure and support Barcelona in the final third.

Since the arrival of Luis Enrique, Iniesta continues in the left-sided center midfield role but now can switch during the game with Neymar, the left forward under Enrique. This places enormous pressure for the opposing right back with Iniesta and Neymar constantly switching from the half space to the flank and vice versa.

One of the main attributes of Iniesta's game, though often unrecognized, is his constant movement off the ball to create spaces for his teammates to move into.

While not a prolific scorer by any means, Iniesta has been able to step up and score goals in the biggest of moments, perhaps none more memorable than the 2010 World Cup winning strike over Holland in extra time of the final.

Iniesta has represented Spain over 100 times in his career and is now approaching 400 league appearances for Barcelona.[20] Besides his obviously ample team awards, Iniesta has always proven to be the player for the big occasions. His influence off the bench during the 2006 Champions League was a match-winning performance, leading Barcelona to the title. Iniesta was named Man of the Match in the World Cup 2010 final, the Euro 2012 final, and the Champions League final in 2015. While never able to break the Ronaldo/Messi Ballon D'Or dominance, Iniesta was voted to a top four finish in three separate years.

---

20   *Ibid.*

DANI ALVES (2008-2016)

The 32-year-old Dani Alves has consistently been one of the top offensive right backs of the last ten years. The Brazilian began his European career when he joined Sevilla in 2002. After six successful seasons of building his reputation as a dynamic full back, Alves moved to Barcelona in 2008. Already a two-time UEFA Cup champion in Seville, the honors were only going to become even more plentiful at the Nou Camp. Alves has now won five La Liga and three Champions League titles among many others. Individually, he has been named in FIFA's Pro XI five times.[21]

In comparison to the frequently changed left back position at Barcelona, the right back position has stayed consistent since Alves's arrival in 2008. Since he joined Barcelona, Alves has always been used as a right back high up the field, providing width in attack. The only aspect that the coaches have tinkered with is how high up the field he is positioned and whether Alves will be used to provide the width on the right side or if he will also be used for underlapping, supporting runs into the half spaces.

Since Luis Enrique's arrival, the right side has been the principle side for Barcelona's build up due to the likes of Alves and Messi operating on the same flank. Depending on Messi's movement, Alves will adjust to him. If Messi is high and wide, Alves will be positioned in the half space to either support from behind or underlap Messi. This allows him to be able to combine with Messi. If Messi drops into his favored right half space, Alves will make an overlapping run, now responsible for providing the width for Barcelona's right hand side.

Alves has been an integral member of the Brazil national squad since his debut in 2006. He was a member of their 2007 Copa America championship side as well being a Confederations Cup champion in 2009 and 2013. Alves has made over 80 appearances in total for his country.

---

21   *Ibid.*

LIONEL MESSI (2003-PRESENT)

Lionel Messi has established himself as not only one of the two greatest players of his generation, but potentially one of the most influential players the sport has ever seen. He has made over 300 appearances in the league for Barcelona since his debut and has an average of one goal per game over the duration of his career. Messi was brought up in the Barcelona youth system and made his debut for the first team in 2003.

Words simply cannot describe the ability Messi has with the ball at his feet. His effectiveness and power has not dwindled throughout his career, despite the many different strategies his opponents have used to stop him.

Early in his career, under Pep Guardiola, Messi would mainly operate as a false number 9. In other words, rather than playing as a center forward between the two opposing center backs and trying to win aerial battles, he would instead drift back into the right half space at midfield and try to collect the ball. If he accomplished this, he would dribble and look to combine with his strong left foot in a 4-3-3 shape. This created disorganization for the opponent as it is extremely difficult to keep a good shape defensively when Messi overloads the right half channel.

Under Luis Enrique in the present, Messi now starts as the right forward, with Suarez as the number 9 position and Dani Alves acting as the support on his side. Messi and Alves are a dynamic duo and are gifted in reading the other's movements. For example, if Messi drifts into the half space from the right side flank, Alves can anticipate providing the width for Messi; if Alves were to go into the right half space then Messi would now provide the width for Alves. They fit together so well because of their extreme adeptness in playing out of intense pressure from the opponent through combination play. Suarez will also drift to the right side from time to time, creating even more of an overload. This is likely the reason for Enrique's preference to play through the right side of the field.

Perhaps Messi's most dangerous skill is his phenomenal dribbling ability. With the ball at his left foot, he is nearly unstoppable due to his impeccable close control, low center of gravity, and lightning acceleration. Messi is far from a selfish player and regularly sets his teammates up for goals, even when he is also in a position to score.

The icing on the cake is his precision at set pieces.

Messi has won La Liga with Barcelona an astonishing seven times, along with four Champions League victories. He has been in the FIFA Pro XI every year since 2007.[22] Messi was awarded the Player of the Tournament at the 2014 World Cup in Brazil, after his Argentina side fell in the final to Germany.

NEYMAR (2013-PRESENT)

Neymar has fully justified the massive reputation he established in his native Brazil prior to his big money move to Barcelona from Santos in 2013. He traditionally operates in one of the front three positions alongside Messi and Luis Suarez. Together, they are seen as one of the most dangerous trios in world soccer today, perhaps even one of the most lethal forward groups of all time.

Neymar typically starts as the left forward under Enrique, making use of his unbelievable 1-v-1 ability. Enrique also gives Neymar permission to dribble inside toward the goal, either looking to score or to combine with Suarez and Messi. Enrique also interchanges Iniesta as the left-sided center midfielder and Neymar as the left winger because both are able to perform in either position at a very high level. These switches at fast speed are incredibly hard to deal with, especially for the opposing right back. This opposing right back needs to make the decision either to mark Neymar and potentially get beaten or to allow Neymar to receive the ball between the defense and midfield lines, ensuring that he stays connected to his back four while not allowing Iniesta to get behind the defensive line.

One of Neymar's unsung talents is his tactical awareness and impeccable timing in making movements toward open space. When receiving the ball in these spaces, Neymar demonstrates his world-class technical skills and explosive initial movements, typically leaving his defender behind. Neymar's lightning quick speed, elusive dribbling skills, and deadly finishes on goal make him a truly dynamic player.

Neymar is also the heartbeat of the current Brazilian national team. He had an outstanding World Cup in 2014, ending after a traumatic back injury before the

---

22   *See Wikipedia.*

semifinals. The depth and degree of his impact with the Brazilian team was noticeable as the team fell apart in the semifinals after his injury ruled him out of the rest of the tournament. Despite his tender age, Neymar has already played 69 times for Brazil, scoring a mesmerizing 46 goals in the process.[23]

LUIS SUAREZ (2014-PRESENT)

In only his second season since joining Barcelona in July 2014, Luis Suarez is already considered one of the most dangerous forwards in world soccer. The 29-year-old Uruguayan international had a modest start to his European journey, playing with the Dutch side of Groningen. From that point on, Suarez quickly moved on to bigger and better things. An outstanding career at Ajax was soon followed by three brilliant seasons at Liverpool where Suarez solidified his reputation as a world-class performer.

Suarez's performance at Liverpool encouraged Barcelona to invest over 90 million Euros to bring him to the Nou Camp. Suarez transitioned seamlessly into the Barcelona attack, completing the dynamic trio alongside Neymar and Messi. In his first season at Barcelona, under Luis Enrique, Suarez started as a right forward, with Messi in the central striker position, or vice versa. During the current 2015-2016 season, Suarez almost exclusively plays as the central striker in all games from the start. During the course of the game, Suarez may transition to the right flank, interchanging with Messi and coming from the right flank to the center forward position.

Suarez will also come to the right half space, overloading that area with Messi and Alves and providing width. Simultaneously, the right center midfielder (typically Rakitic) will move to the central forward position. Enrique trusts Suarez and the rest of his team to interchange while ensuring all strategic areas on the field are covered; this demonstrates the degree of tactical awareness each player must possess in order to play for Enrique's Barcelona.

On top of his fantastic movement off the ball, Suarez is truly a brilliant, modern day number 9. He can score all types of goals, although he has a particular knack for the screamers—the spectacular goals from distance—and has dizzying dribbling skills. A primary strength of Suarez is his tireless work ethic, never giving the defenders a

---

23   *Ibid.*

moment's rest. This is a great fit for Barcelona's high pressing and counter pressing game. Suarez plays the game with a youthful endeavor and effort rarely seen in flair players. He is lethal with free kicks and is a danger to score from any position on the field within 35 yards of goal.

Suarez has been an overall dominating force for his country, having played over 80 times and scoring 43 goals.[24] The Uruguayan National Team reached the World Cup semifinals in 2010, and won the 2011 Copa America with Suarez in the team.

GENERAL SETUP UNDER LUIS ENRIQUE

OFFENSIVE

As one would expect from a former Barcelona player, Luis Enrique's focus primarily revolves around dominating through possession, but he also utilizes a more direct attacking approach when necessary. This approach gives him the best use of his three world-class forwards (Messi, Neymar, and Suarez) when the opportunity presents itself.

When Barcelona is in clear possession of the ball, the center backs spread to encompass the width of the penalty box, and the outside backs push forward. A primary piece of this is that Alves (right outside back) provides the width and will push higher compared to Alba (left outside back), who will provide deeper support more so than width.

Busquets serves as the midfield anchor. He attempts to receive the ball in the holding midfield area, or, if marked, he will drop between the two center backs in order to start the attack from the back. Iniesta (left midfield) will then position himself either in the left half space or provide width by transitioning to the wing. This will typically happen if Neymar drops to the left half space. Either Turan or Rakitic typically plays the right midfield position. Either of these players makes vertical movements to support Messi from the half space or to push forward next to Suarez in order to open the half space

---

24   See *Wikipedia*.

for Messi to drift into. Suarez, mainly the center forward, will often drop back between the midfield and defensive line of the opponent in order to combine or create space in behind the defensive line. Suarez is also able to switch positions with Messi, becoming the right winger as Messi transitions to high forward.

Luis Enrique's preferred side to attack from is the right side with Messi, Suarez, and Alves. However, if the opponent shifts to cover the right, Messi is more than capable of switching the ball with his left foot to Neymar (forward) to create a 1-v-1 opportunity on the left side.

A frequent tactic that is observed is Suarez, Messi, and Neymar drifting to the middle of the field and keeping the opposing back four busy, thus creating space on the outside channels. This space can now be exploited, and the opposing outside midfielder must now make a decision: focus on Barcelona's center midfielders in the offensive half space or focus on their outside backs moving high up the field. Barcelona is now able to overload the flanks when the three forwards are positioned so close together in the middle.

In conclusion, when Barcelona attacks, it is clear that Enrique is attempting to capitalize on the individual quality of the players regarding general team tactics. He is also comfortable allowing Suarez, Messi, and Neymar to take the ball and perform with their unquestionable individual brilliance.

DEFENSIVE

It was evident right from the outset that Luis Enrique was returning to the successful pressing strategy introduced by Guardiola. However, Enrique started to press even higher up the field by sending multiple players toward the opposing player in possession of the ball as soon as the ball was played to the outside channels of the field. Simultaneously, when the ball moved to the central zone, Barcelona became more compact in order to force the ball to the side.

Barcelona's style of pressing is highly aggressive, not just in the way that they press the opposition player on the ball but also in the manner in which they position themselves to block the passing lanes for the opposition.

It can be difficult to determine Enrique's defensive approach due to such a highly aggressive pressing style as well as the way the opposing teams attempt to defend against Barcelona. Many teams will position their whole team, maybe leaving one player high, on top of their own defensive box and await Barcelona there. Because of this, Barcelona will either win the ball back via counter-pressing (trying to win the ball back immediately after losing possession) or winning the long ball that the other team is trying to counter with.

When the opposing team is able to have controlled possession and build up from the back, Suarez (center forward) will aim to split the two opposing center backs, take away the option to switch the field of play, and force the play down one side of the field. When this occurs, the other Barcelona players will shift to the ball-side of the field to press the player in possession as well as taking all possible outlets on the side of the ball away.

Enrique also trains Barcelona to keep a high defensive line, regardless of whether they have pressure on the opposing player on the ball or not. The Barcelona back four tend to maintain incredible compactness horizontally. The reason for this is the need to keep the field as compact as possible, due to their aggressive pressing style. This limits the spaces between the vertical lines. Additionally, keeping a high defensive line even without pressuring the ball melds well with Barcelona's strengths, primarily the incredible speeds of Barcelona's back four.

When Barcelona is forced to defend deep in their own third, Enrique is willing to take more risks than previous Barcelona coaches. He allows Messi, Suarez, and Neymar to stay high while the other seven (back four and three center midfielders) players defend in a 4-3 shape.

Barcelona's defensive strategy can be summarized as aggressive, evidenced by keeping the back four high even after losing the possession of the ball. When they do defend, they will typically use the back four and the three midfield players, keeping the three forwards high. Many teams have come to respect this because the three forwards are just so dangerous on the break. The opposing team may decide to keep more numbers back to defend against these three forwards. However, this system is not without risk in keeping such a high line, especially if the opposing team decides to push more numbers forward in attack.

CASE STUDY #1:
A BARCELONA WIN

February 3, 2016

Player Lineups for FC Barcelona (red) vs. Valencia CF (white) (with player tendencies)

Barcelona vs. Valencia CF

7:0

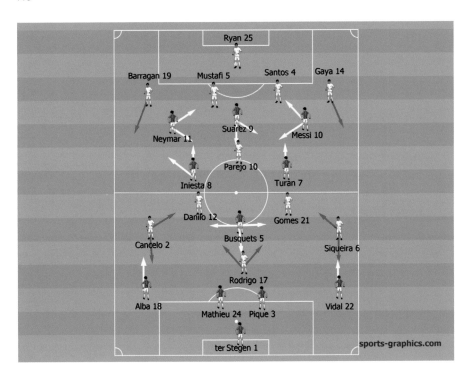

12 SECONDS

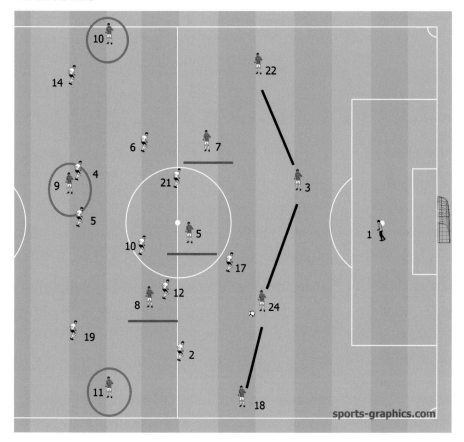

Barcelona's shape is evident when they are in clear possession; when in possession of the ball, Barcelona is attempting to spread out as much as possible. Messi and Neymar are providing full width with Suarez (red circles) stretching the defense as much as possible. Barcelona is following the rules of positional play by keeping no more than two players in a vertical line and no more than three in a horizontal line. That's why the Barcelona midfielders (blue) are positioned in a way that offers great passing angles. They constantly move in sync with the opposition and the ball to maintain those angles. Valencia is set up with five midfielders to keep the midfield as compact as possible. Barcelona center back Mathieu simply takes this space and dribbles out, moving the Valencia players and forcing them to adjust to his dribbling.

17 SECONDS

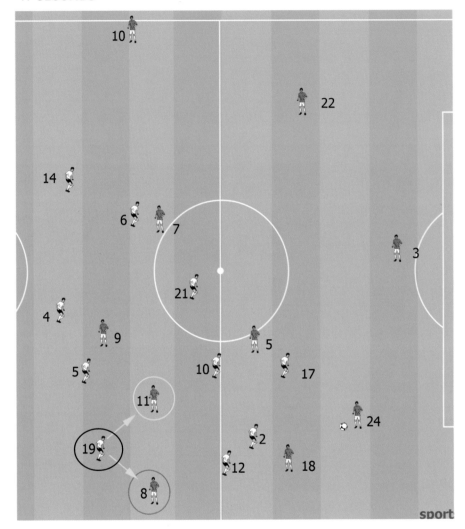

Only five seconds later, every player continues to take care of their channel of the field. However, if you look closely, you will see that Barcelona players drift into specific spaces while at the same time ensuring that a different player will occupy the space that has just been vacated. Remember, there are certain pairs who interchange constantly in this system. Iniesta (red) and Neymar (yellow) have switched and Neymar now drops into the midfield half space while Iniesta provides the width in the channel. This causes problems for Valencia's defenders, as the right back must now make a decision. He must decide whether to leave Neymar to watch for Iniesta's potential run in behind, or to follow Neymar to prevent him from receiving the ball at his feet, possibly allowing Iniesta to get the ball in behind him.

10 MINUTES, 58 SECONDS

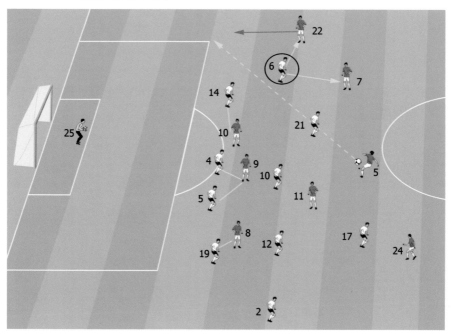

In this picture, you can see the types of problems that Barcelona gives other teams due to the movements that Barcelona players display as they push forward. All three forwards from Barcelona drift inside, the two center midfielders sit in the half spaces, and the right outside back (red arrow) makes an overlapping run.

Valencia's back four are now occupied by Barcelona's three forwards: Messi (between the outside back and left center back), Suarez (between the two center backs), and Iniesta (between the right center back and right back). Valencia attempts to shrink the spaces between their back four to monitor Messi, Suarez, and Iniesta. This horizontal compactness in the back four creates huge spaces in the outside channels. Vidal (Barcelona outside back) runs into this space after Valencia fails to place pressure on the ball carrier. The ball carrier can now either leisurely play the ball into that space for Vidal or make a short pass into the right half space, creating a 2-v-1 overload on the right side.

28 MINUTES, 19 SECONDS

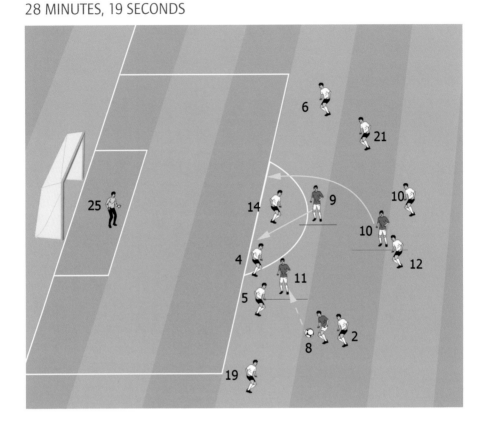

One of the main factors contributing to the dangerousness of Barcelona's offense is the sheer quality that their three strikers have in speed, dribbling, linking up play, finishing, and pure creativity. On top of this talent, Enrique also gives them the freedom to express themselves on the ball. In this picture, Neymar (red) receives the ball from Iniesta, then back-heels it to Suarez (blue). Suarez pretends to receive it in order to draw in the defenders to him. He leaves the ball for Messi, who is running into the space just created by Suarez. Messi takes one touch and, with the outside of his foot, chips the ball into the left side netting.

24 MINUTES, 28 SECONDS

When in transition from offense to defense, Barcelona immediately tries to win the ball back. In other words, when they lose the ball, they aggressively go at the ball carrier with multiple players. Simultaneously, other Barcelona players work to close down the opposition's outlets by blocking passing lanes. In this picture, Barcelona lost possession and within seconds, multiple Barcelona players (red) placed immediate pressure on the ball. Simultaneously, they reduce potential options for Valencia players to receive the ball (yellow). The Barcelona players have created defensive shadows that now block passing lanes for Valencia.

36 MINUTES

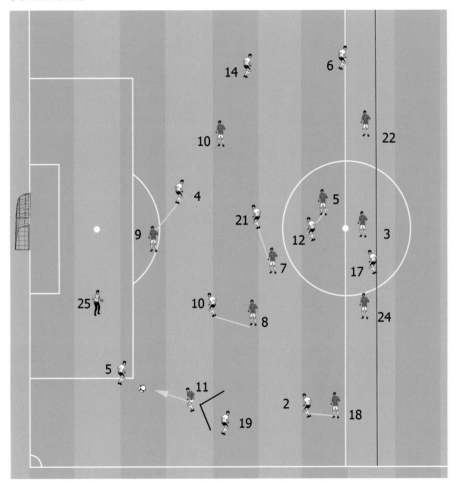

In this picture, you can see that Valencia tries to build out of the back by spreading their players after escaping the Barcelona pressure. The role of the Barcelona center forward is to split the two Valencia center backs, forcing them to play down ball-side so the rest of the Barcelona team can shift over. Barcelona's outside forward then places the Valencia outside back in his defensive shadow (blocking passing options) and sprints toward the player in possession, placing pressure on him. At the same time, the other Barcelona players all move to the side of the ball and limit the potential passing options for the Valencia player. Barcelona tries to hold a high line, creating as much compactness as possible with the rest of the team.

2 MINUTES, 11 SECONDS

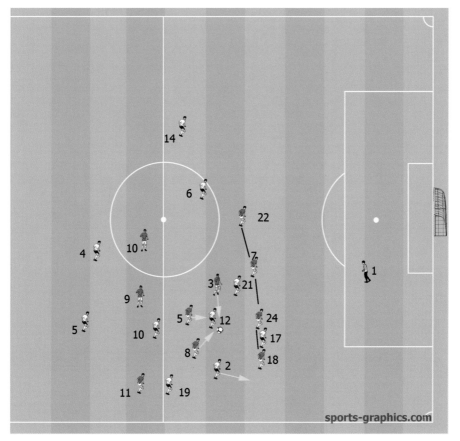

This picture shows the incredibly high line Barcelona keeps, allowing them to be as compact as possible between the midfield and the defensive line. The high pressing and counter-pressing game that Barcelona utilizes requires compactness to prevent the other team from taking advantage of the spaces in between the lines to combine with one another to get out of Barcelona's pressing. The Barcelona back four maintain horizontal compactness wherever the ball is. The roles of each player is clear in this picture: when there is no pressure on the ball, the back four drop together while the Barcelona midfielders back-press the Valencia player with the ball.

2 MINUTES, 19 SECONDS

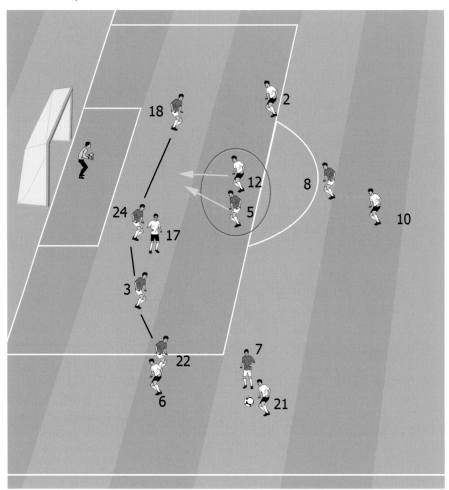

When Barcelona defend deep and Valencia play out of their pressure, Barcelona defend with their back four and the three midfielders, leaving Messi, Neymar, and Suarez high. This forces Valencia to make a decision as to how many additional players they push up when they are constructing the attack. The Barcelona back four will usually be pretty far over to the ball-side to stay as connected to each other as possible.

 Here the Barcelona back four move over to ball-side, including the right-sided central midfielder (Turan.) This creates a hole in their back four, because Barcelona's left back could not stay connected to the rest of the back four; instead Turan needs to look out for Valencia's right winger. Valencia's center midfield player tries to exploit that space, but Busquets (red) is well aware of his surroundings and position, and is therefore able to fill the hole created in the back four, easily covering the cross from Valencia.

CASE STUDY #2:
BEATING BARCELONA

April 20, 2011

Player Lineups for FC Barcelona (red) vs. Real Madrid (white) (with player tendencies)

FC Barcelona vs. Real Madrid

0:1

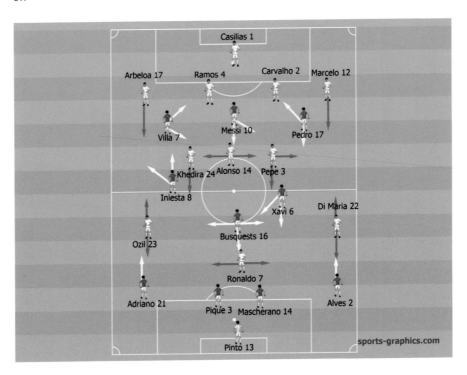

18 SECONDS

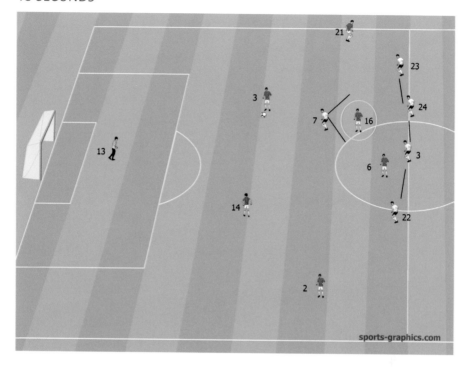

Real Madrid did not high press Barcelona, waiting patiently around the midfield area instead while staying as compact as possible.

When Barcelona build from the back, Madrid defend in a 1-4-1-4-1 shape where individual players have specific tasks that are not usually typical of Real Madrid's setup. Ronaldo is now responsible for blocking the Barcelona center backs' passing lanes to Busquets.

As this picture demonstrates, when Piqué has the ball, Busquets (yellow) is in Ronaldo's defensive shadow and thus unable to receive the ball. As a result, the Barcelona center backs can only use horizontal passes and must keep the ball within their back line. If they dribble forward with the ball, Ronaldo will continue to block off the passing lane to Busquets while also attacking the center back who is trying to dribble out of the back at full speed.

23 SECONDS

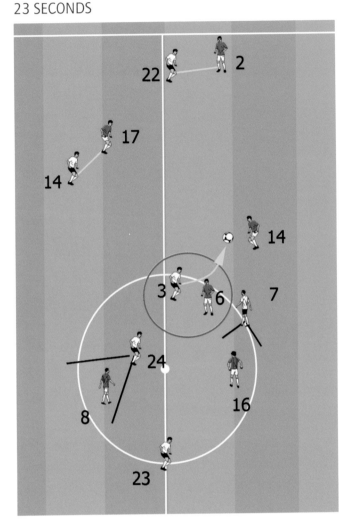

Mourinho identifies Xavi as one of the major players in Barcelona's buildup. So Pepe (Real Madrid), who is quite an aggressive physical presence, marks Xavi all over the field, effectively disrupting the Barcelona buildup. This picture shows that Pepe only leaves Xavi to put him in his defensive shadow while pressuring a different Barcelona player. This triggers the other Madrid players to close off the other passing options for the player now under pressure by Pepe. This tactic either forces the long ball, where Madrid has a height advantage, or forces a short pass into one of the marked players with the aim of winning the ball back higher up the field to counter attack right away.

17 MINUTES, 18 SECONDS

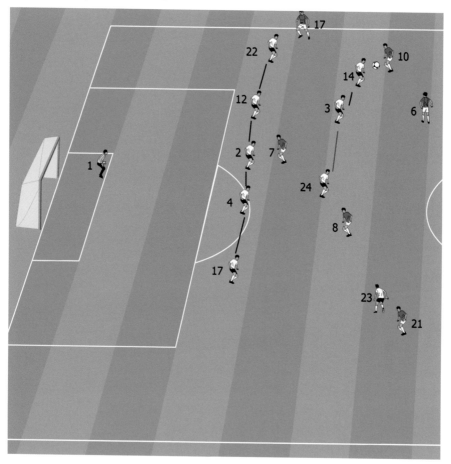

When Barcelona bypasses the Madrid midfield pressing, forcing them to defend deep, their shape looks like a 1-4-4-2 / 1-5-3-2, depending on how high Barcelona push their outside back who is ball-side. This influences how deep Madrid's winger will defend.

In this picture, Madrid defends with their three central midfielders (Alonso, Pepe, and Khedira—green line) all of whom push to ball-side to prevent Barcelona from combining in the offensive half space on the side of the ball. The Madrid back four are set zonally and the left forward (ball-side forward) comes all the way back to join the back four, keeping Barcelona's outside back from getting in behind him. This leaves Ronaldo and the right forward high, allowing them to transition quickly into the holes Barcelona then leaves, creating goal-scoring opportunities in the transition from defense to offense. This makes the normal 4-4-2 shape into a 5-3-2 shape defensively.

55 MINUTES, 17 SECONDS

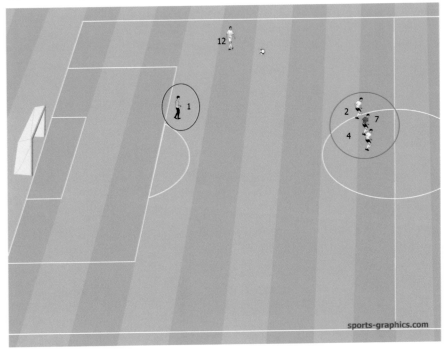

Madrid accurately identifies Barcelona's strengths in their pressing and counter-pressing game as well as their weakness at winning second balls.

As a result, Madrid aims every free kick or goal kick as far up the field as possible, making it extraordinarily difficult for Barcelona to win the ball back in Madrid's half and play their normal pressing game. Marcelo (Real Madrid) has plenty of space to build up with Casillas (Real Madrid goalkeeper) but he instead chooses to send the ball long. Madrid then look to win the first ball. Even if they don't win the first ball, players like Khedira and Pepe are known to be good fighters for the second ball. By going long and then trying to create those second ball battles, the game becomes scrappy, resulting in a loss of flow and suiting Madrid better than Barcelona. Even if Barcelona wins the ball, it is still in their half and they have to work the ball up the field. This differs from Barcelona's normal game where they usually win the ball in the opposition's half, leaving a shorter distance to the opponent's goal.

58 MINUTES, 30 SECONDS

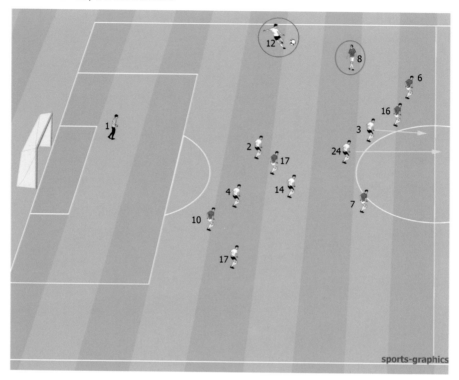

Even when there is no pressure on the ball, Marcelo, who is a great passer and dribbler, still chooses to go long in open play (not just on set pieces). Iniesta (green) does not try to pressure and press because he knows Marcelo (red) will just go long. The other Madrid players at the back, who could provide support for a short buildup, stay away. Pepe and Khedira are already on their way up the field to position themselves for the second ball, all before Marcelo (green) has even played the ball.

2 MINUTES, 45 SECONDS

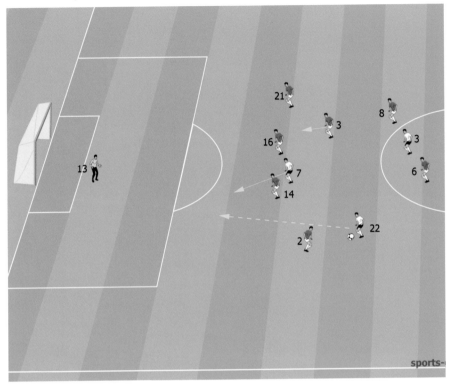

One of Real Madrid's attacking strategies after winning the ball is to penetrate in the final third of the field with as much vertical passing as possible. This is due to Barcelona's aggressive style of defending, which can open up space behind the defense for Real Madrid players to run into.

With the speed and dribbling ability of Ronaldo as the lone striker, Di Maria as the left winger, and the great passing skills of Mesut Özil as the right winger, Madrid is set up for an attacking strategy.

After Madrid win the ball and find Di Maria with a quick pass forward, Barcelona keeps their high line, which Ronaldo is looking to exploit with his run in behind.

11 MINUTES, 34 SECONDS

When Real Madrid attacks and Barcelona is defending deep in their box, both Khedira and Pepe join Ronaldo with runs from the midfield because both are great headers of the ball. This strategy creates mismatches against the smaller, less athletic players from Barcelona. When attacking down the flanks, Madrid pushes their outside backs high up to support the wingers. Alonso becomes responsible for stopping or slowing down the counter attack by Barcelona. Pushing multiple center midfielders into Barcelona's box allows Madrid to create mismatches and additionally overload in the box. Barcelona defends by overloading players around the ball which leaves them with fewer players to defend away from the ball. Thus when Madrid crosses the ball, they are always aimed for the back post where Khedira and Pepe are waiting to go up against a smaller Barcelona outside back. Madrid had multiple good scoring opportunities by using this tactic.

FC BAYERN MUNICH

HISTORY

FC Bayern Munich was founded in 1900 and has been established as one of the European super powers in soccer. The team possesses not only the highest number of Bundesliga titles, but also the most European titles of any other German club team, solidifying their status as the most successful German club team in history.[25] FC Bayern Munich began to experience their best run in 1996 and have been at the height of success throughout the past 20 years. During this time, they have won twelve league titles and nine DFB Pokal titles (which is a German knockout soccer cup competition held annually). Additional jewels in their crown have been two UEFA Champions League titles (2000-2001 and 2012-2013) in the past twenty years.

FC Bayern Munich is based in Munich, a city located in the south of Germany and, with a population of over 1.3 million people, is one of the biggest cities in the country. Allianz Arena, built in 2005, is where they call home and seats just over 75,000 fans for every game. The club is privately owned through various stock holdings, including pieces owned by Adidas, Audi, and Volkswagen. As is the tradition of soccer, Bayern is not without rivalries. Their two biggest rivals include Borussia Dortmund and FC Nurnberg, with the match against Nurnberg typically being called the Bavarian Derby. The club has over 3,000 supporting fan clubs across the globe and is one of the most famous clubs in the world. Their more famous supporters include Pope Benedict XVI and Boris Becker.

---

25   See Wikipedia.

Team Motto: *Mia san Mia. ("We are who we are.")*

HONORS

- ★ 25 Bundesliga Titles
- ★ 17 DFB Cup Titles
- ★ 5 European Cup/Champions League Titles
- ★ 1 UEFA Cup
- ★ 1 UEFA Cup Winners Cup
- ★ 1 UEFA Super Cup
- ★ 2 Intercontinental Cups
- ★ 1 FIFA World Club Cup

FC BAYERN MUNICH COACHES

LOUIS VAN GAAL (2009-2011)

The 64-year-old Dutchman, currently managing Manchester United, was in charge at Bayern Munich from 2009-2011. Louis van Gaal spent the majority of his own playing career at Sparta Rotterdam, making a total of 331 appearances throughout his 15-year playing career.[26] An interesting fact about van Gaal is that he has also spent time as a physical education instructor.

Prior to leading FC Bayern Munich, van Gaal managed various teams that included Ajax (1991-1997, 2004), Barcelona (1997-2000, 2002-2003), AZ Alkmaar (2005-2009), and the Netherlands National Team (2000-2002, 2012-2014). His longest and most successful tenure as a head coach was at his first club, Ajax, where he managed the team for six seasons. During this time, he led Ajax to win the Eredivisie League Title three years in a row (1993-1995) and the UEFA Champions League Title (1994-1995). Louis van Gaal's arrival at Bayern followed one of the least successful periods in the history of the club. Fortunately, he was not afraid to make major changes in the team's system of play. Van Gaal is systems-oriented in his coaching approach and

---

26   *Ibid.*

typically doesn't adjust to the team's current style of play. Therefore he recruits players based on specific profiles that he deems appropriate for fitting into his system.

His legend is that of a great tactical coach who is confident in his opinions. He discharged certain players and imposed a clear strategy of his style of play. New players were signed under van Gaal as well as players who were promoted from the Bayern youth academy. Many of the Bayern players enjoyed learning van Gaal's approach to the game due to his focus on the individual strengths of each player as well as striving to have the majority of possession in matches. This approach saw Bayern winning the Bundesliga in his first season as head coach. The majority of the players who played for him continue to compete for Bayern Munich. Those key players include Thomas Müller, Arjen Robben, Franck Ribéry, Philipp Lahm, Holger Badstuber, David Alaba, and Manuel Neuer. Van Gaal is renowned for his somewhat challenging personality, which likely influences his quick, short stay at a club if he does not bring success. When this inevitably occurred, the club decided to bring back Jupp Heynckes for his third spell at Bayern.

HONORS AT FC BAYERN MUNICH
★ Bundesliga Title: 1
★ DFB Pokal: 1
★ DFL Supercup: 1

JUPP HEYNCKES (2011-2013)

The former head coach of Bayern Munich, nicknamed "Osram" for his typically reddish face on the sidelines, is of German descent and turned 71 in May 2016. The majority of his playing career was spent at Borussia Mönchengladbach, where he played in two separate spells for a total of twelve seasons. He made almost 400 appearances during his club career and played 39 times for West Germany. He is ranked third among the top goal scorers in the history of the Bundesliga, with 220 total goals scored.[27] Heynckes had an impressive playing career, including winning the Bundesliga title on four occasions, the DFB Pokal cup once, and the World Cup in 1974 with West Germany.

---

27 Ibid.

He began his managerial career in 1979 with Borussia Mönchengladbach, the club that he used to play for. This was his longest tenure, and he spent eight seasons with this team. After his time at Mönchengladbach, he bounced around various clubs over the next 24 years, including Bayern Munich, Athletic Bilbao, Real Madrid, Schalke, and Bayer Leverkusen, before returning to Bayern Munich one last time (2011-2013) before retirement. He led Real Madrid to the UEFA Champions League title in 1997-1998 although he experienced the most coaching success during his 2012-2013 stint with Bayern Munich. It was during this time that the team completed the treble by winning the Bundesliga title, the UEFA Champions League, and the DFB-Pokal.

Heynckes's coaching philosophy focuses on balance, both offensively and defensively. He stepped in after van Gaal left, and was fortunate enough to inherit a team in great shape. Bayern Munich possessed a clear philosophy and was a strong collective unit, so Heynckes needed only to tweak the system. He did this by bringing in a few players of his own.

Some of the main tactical changes that he made were to place the defensive side at a much higher priority. No matter if it was Robben or Müller, each player needed to work defensively and participate in counter-pressing, even more than was required under van Gaal. Though Heynckes's goal was to have the majority of possession in the game, he also ensured that options for a quick transition were available through players such as Robben and Ribéry, who were on the wings and had the license to take risks.

With regards to the tactical system, he continued with the 4-2-3-1 adopted by van Gaal when in possession of the ball. However, the way Bayern Munich pressed was adapted to the individual team they were playing.

HONORS AT FC BAYERN MUNICH
★ UEFA Champions League: 1
★ Bundesliga Title: 3
★ DFB Pokal: 1
★ DFL Supercup: 1

JOSEP "PEP" GUARDIOLA (2013-2016)

The 45-year-old Spanish native spent a majority of his playing career at Barcelona, where he made over 250 appearances for the team and won seven league titles. He went on to play at various clubs before retiring as a player in 2006. During his playing career, Pep made 47 appearances for the Spanish National team and assisted his team in winning a gold medal at the 1992 Olympics.[28] Pep Guardiola started his coaching career with the Barcelona "B" team. After a year of success with the second team, Pep was quickly promoted to head coach of Barcelona and enjoyed four years of undoubted success between 2008 and 2012. In his first season as head coach, he won both the Copa del Rey and La Liga titles. He finished this hugely successful first year by also winning the UEFA Champions League, thus completing the treble. The remaining three years saw his team win ten other domestic and European honors including the 2010-2011 UEFA Champions League. Pep's dominating style throughout his short spell as head coach of Barcelona triggered many soccer experts to identify his group of players as one of the best teams in the history of soccer. Since leaving Barcelona, he has continued to build upon his reputation as a tactically aggressive coach by bringing similar success to FC Bayern Munich. Guardiola arrived at FC Bayern on June 26, 2013 and has since led them to two Bundesliga titles in the last two seasons. Pep's philosophy is based on the three Ps: position, possession, and play.

HONORS AT FC BAYERN MUNICH
★   Bundesliga Title: 2
★   DFB Pokal: 1
★   UEFA Super Cup: 1
★   FIFA Club World Cup: 1

---

28   Ibid.

FC BAYERN MUNICH KEY PLAYERS

MANUEL NEUER (2011-PRESENT)

Manuel Neuer, who signed from Schalke 04 after the 2010-2011 season, is considered to be the best goalkeeper in the world. Neuer also has over 60 caps for the German national team and won the World Cup in Brazil in 2014 as the starting goalkeeper. He won the German Footballer of the Year Award (2011, 2014), FIFA World Cup Golden Gloves Award (2014), and placed 3rd for the Ballon d'Or voting (2014). All his accomplishments are even more impressive considering he is only 29 years old, the prime age for a goalkeeper.

Physically, he is an imposing 6'4" and weighs around 200 pounds. Mentally and physically he is a goalkeeper who tends to be highly proactive when coming out for crosses or set pieces. This characteristic has been constant for Neuer with every coach he has played under during his time at Bayern. His tremendous skills on the ball consistently give Bayern great outlets to start building up from the back. Under Jupp Heynckes, who played a slightly more direct and transitional game, Neuer was able to showcase his long throw and long ball to start the buildup for Bayern. This has changed somewhat under Pep, who prefers to use him in Bayern's buildup play out of the back. Bayern Munich also plays a high line with the counter-pressing system that Pep has instilled, so Neuer is ultimately a sweeper-keeper. Jupp Heynckes instilled a great pressing game, especially during his last season with Bayern, but Pep takes an even riskier approach. In this role, Neuer often needs to clear the ball by using his head or feet in order to stay connected to his team as he is often a long way outside his box. This demonstrates Neuer's elite tactical awareness and the trust that his coach has in him to be proactive.

PHILIPP LAHM (2002-PRESENT)

Philipp Lahm is the current captain of the club, having made over 300 appearances in the Bundesliga for Bayern. Lahm joined the club 14 years ago after making his first appearance in November 2002. The 32-year-old Lahm was also captain of Germany when they won the World Cup in 2014. He retired after making 113 appearances for the national team.

Guardiola has said that Lahm is one of the best pure soccer players that he has ever coached. That is high praise from a coach who has worked with players such as Xavi, Andrés Iniesta, and Lionel Messi.

Lahm's role within this particular Bayern team has changed significantly. This change started under van Gaal and Heynckes, who both used Lahm as either the right back or the left back for the team. Lahm has never been shy about acknowledging his preference of playing right back over left back. Lahm broke into Bayern's first team and the German national side as a left back, even though he was stronger on his right foot. The main problem with Lahm on the left side is that he has to cross the ball with his weaker foot, a skill that he is not well-known for. Therefore, when playing on the left side, he drifts infield, decreasing the width on his side as well as leaving holes in behind him. Teams tried to exploit this by attacking the empty space. Jupp Heynckes recognized the problem and fixed it by filling that space with one of the holding midfielders. However, this is still not Lahm's ideal position. In the first two seasons under Pep, Lahm has been playing as a right back or center midfielder. In the current season, Lahm plays both roles concurrently. In other words, Lahm plays as a right back when the other team is in possession, but when Bayern has possession, he moves into the center midfield position to create a 3-2-4-1 shape for Bayern. Some of Lahm's main attributes are that he is a solid decision maker under intense pressure and possesses exceptional passing skills. Lahm is also an incredible defender in 1-v-1 situations.

JEROME BOATENG (2011-PRESENT)

Jerome Boateng is one of the undoubted leaders of the current Bayern Munich team, which has been a role that he has grown into since his arrival in July 2011 from Manchester City. Boateng has been the starting right center back since 2011-2012. His leadership, accompanied by his technical and tactical ability, has grown tremendously over the last five years. He now has over 120 Bundesliga appearances under these top coaches, and is one of the first names on Pep's team sheet. Boateng has made fast progress with his tactical awareness and positional play under the guidance of Pep. He is one of the most physically imposing center backs in the world with the combination of his size (6'4"), speed, and aggression. Boateng is of the reasons that Pep can play such a risky counter-pressing system. Even if the opponent does get in behind Bayern, Boateng has the recovery pace to catch up, even to the fastest forwards in the Bundesliga.

An interesting fact about Boateng is that he and fellow soccer player, Kevin Prince-Boateng, are half-brothers. They are both dual citizens of Ghana and Germany. Kevin Prince-Boateng competes for the Ghanaian National team and Jerome ties his boots for Germany. Jerome was also a part of the World Cup Championship German team in 2014 and has over 50 caps for his country.

DAVID ALABA (2011-PRESENT)

David Alaba is without a doubt one of the best (perhaps even THE best) left back in the world. He is only 23 years old, but has been a regular fixture for Bayern since he was 19 years old. He began his Bayern career after his first team debut in February of 2011 and has since played over 120 times for Bayern. Alaba has played his entire senior career with Bayern Munich, with the exception of the 2011 season when he went on loan to Hoffenheim. Unlike the other four defenders at Bayern, Alaba does not play for the German national team. He is an Austrian national and operates in the playmaking role for his national team. He played his youth career at both SV Aspern and Austria Wien. The 5'11" Alaba has been named as the Austrian Footballer of the Year from 2011 to 2015.[29]

---

29   *See Wikipedia.*

Alaba began to see playing time as a left back under van Gaal but turned into a regular starter under the guidance of Jupp Heynckes. Heynckes placed a high degree of trust in Alaba to use his speed as an overlapping outside back in a 4-2-3-1 system. Alaba also provided width and backwards support to Ribéry, who is known to dribble and cut inside on most occasions.

Alaba's role under Pep has changed slightly. Pep is a great admirer of Alaba, which is evident in the roles he has entrusted to him in the last two seasons. Alaba's different roles include left back, center back, holding midfield, offensive midfield, and left midfield. He also possesses great speed and technical skills. He is a very aggressive player, especially in 1-v-1 defensive situations. Underlying his exceptional ability to be effective in so many roles, Alaba possesses a tremendous tactical ability, possibly one of the best in the world. Alaba defies the stereotypical roles of a left back. When playing in this left back position, he is not content to just support the winger and every once in a while make overlapping runs; much like Lahm on the right side, Alaba transitions to the center midfield position from the outside position, providing width if the winger goes inside. If Alaba plays with a player like Coman, he usually underlaps and makes supporting runs into the opposition's box.

THOMAS MÜLLER (2008-PRESENT)

The 6'1" Thomas Müller made his first appearance for Bayern in August 2008 and has since made over 200 Bundesliga appearances. He has close to 70 caps for the German national team and was an integral member of the squad that won the 2014 World Cup, all of this by the age of 26. Müller broke onto the international scene during the 2010 World Cup, where he won the Golden Boot for most goals and most assists, and he was also named the Best Young Player. He is one of three players with at least five goals in each of his first two World Cups (the other two are Miroslav Klose and Teofilo Cubillas). When seeing Müller on the street, your first thought would likely not be that he is a world-class athlete. However, he is certainly one of the best players in the Bundesliga and for the German national team. He has also become the face of Bayern Munich alongside Philipp Lahm since the departure of Bastian Schweinsteiger from the club.

Müller's breakthrough came under van Gaal, who played him mostly on the right wing so that he could provide width when the ball was on his side. Müller also had the freedom to drift into the box due to his amazing feel for finding space. Under Jupp Heynckes's watch, Müller developed into a highly versatile player, playing the left wing position, in behind the striker, and his traditional right midfield position. Müller today, under Pep, is used in a variety of different positions depending on the particular needs of the team that day. He is mainly used as the lone striker or the number 10 position, but he occasionally comes from the right midfield, representative of his role for the German national team and for the two former Bayern Munich coaches.

Müller has almost unparalleled movement in and around the penalty box and seems to have a natural feel for finding the right spot, which makes it possible for him to play in a variety of offensive positions within the many different systems that Pep has instilled. Finally, when Müller does receive the ball, he is one of the deadliest finishers around as well as being capable of finding a better-positioned teammate.

FRANCK RIBÉRY (2007-PRESENT)

The 5'11", 32-year-old French national team player joined Bayern Munich in August 2009 after a successful spell with Olympique Marseille. Franck Ribéry has enjoyed a decorated career playing for his country and has represented France 90 times.

Ribéry, a right-footed player, has played on the left side for all his coaches at Bayern. This idea originally came from van Gaal, who wanted to make use of Ribéry's particular dribbling ability to the inside in a 1-v-1 situation and look to finish with his dangerous shooting ability. Ribéry was a great player for van Gaal, but he did not need to work on his defensive skills as much under him and Van Gaal's way of playing gave him less offensive freedom.

When Jupp Heynckes arrived at Bayern, Ribéry continued in this position for the same offensive reasons, but he needed to focus more on his defensive play and work ethic to become a great player both on and off the ball. Jupp Heynckes' way of playing was a little more direct and focused on moments of transition as well as possession, which was perfect for Ribéry's natural style. After winning the treble during Heynckes' last year at Bayern, Ribéry was voted as the third best player in the world by FIFA (2013). Since the arrival of Pep, Ribéry has had a difficult time adjusting to Pep's philosophy of possessing the ball for longer stretches while looking for the perfect moment to attack as well as battling many injuries. However, when he is healthy, Ribéry continues to play to his strengths on the left side by dribbling inside to finish on his stronger foot.

ARJEN ROBBEN (2009-PRESENT)

The 32-year-old Dutch international previously played for Chelsea and Real Madrid before joining Bayern in August 2009, and has since appeared in over 130 Bundesliga games. Arjen Robben has also been a constant performer for the Netherlands at the big tournaments. He has played for his country 88 times, with the highlight of finishing in second place at the 2010 World Cup. Robben was also recognized by FIFA during the year Bayern won the treble, placing fourth (just behind Neuer) in the voting for the Ballon D'Or in 2014.

Robben's story is very similar to that of Franck Ribéry, in that he has played in the same position under the past three coaches, which is not typically the norm at Bayern. This is quite the contrary for other players such as Lahm, Müller, and Alaba who are utilized in different positions. Robben's amazing speed and unbelievable shooting capability with his left foot are just too much to handle for defenders all over the world. It is no secret that his greatest weapon as a player is to receive the ball at speed on his right. When he gets close to the box, he then cuts in on his stronger left foot to try and shoot. Although this strength is evident, few have found a way to consistently shackle him.

Under both van Gaal and Pep, the ball is kept on one side of the field to then be quickly switched to Robben's side, creating a 1-v-1 matchup. This tactic has been highly successful for Robben as he can show off his dribbling skills. Similar to Ribéry, his most successful time as a Bayern player was under Jupp Heynckes due to the higher use of the transitional approach and the creation of more space for Robben to exploit. However, the opportunities to exploit and run into open space is not as frequent for Robben under Pep because since his arrival at Bayern they have been so dominant in possession that most teams prefer to set up nine or ten players on their own box, which reduces the amount of open space for Robben.

ROBERT LEWANDOWSKI (2014-PRESENT)

Robert Lewandowski is a newer fixture for Bayern, joining the club in July 2014. However, when thinking about great clubs with great strikers, the 26-year-old Polish national player and Bayern Munich danger man is one of the first that comes to mind. After leaving Borussia Dortmund where he developed into one of the best players in the Bundesliga, Lewandowski has played over 50 times in the league for Bayern. Under Pep, he has grown into the complete striker during the last two seasons. He is considered to be one of the top ten best European forwards in the present day. Although Lewandowski is the quickest foreign player to reach 100 goals in the Bundesliga, there is much more to him as a player than just scoring goals. He is also the captain of the Polish National team where he has over 70 caps and was named the Polish player of the year for four consecutive years (2011-2014).[30]

What makes Lewandowski so great is that his ability and range of scoring is immense and diverse. At 6 feet tall, he possesses a tremendous vertical leap, creating a constant threat in the air. Lewandowski also has a powerful shot with both his left and right foot, and it can be difficult to determine which side is his strongest. Perhaps his strongest attribute is his brilliant instincts around the penalty box and his clinical performance in front of the goal. Pep typically does not favor playing with a pure center forward as they typically lack the technical ability necessary for his system. However, this is not a problem with Lewandowski, which is just another reason why he is a cut above an average number 9.

---

30   *See Wikipedia.*

GENERAL SETUP UNDER PEP GUARDIOLA

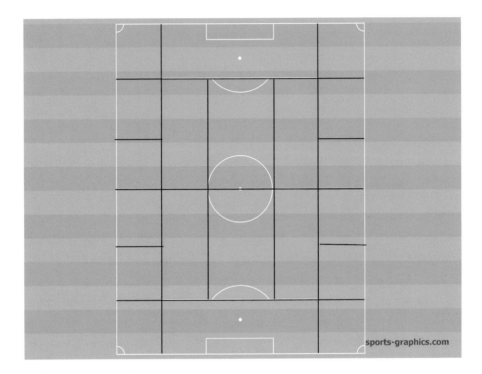

sports-graphics.com

Bayern Munich under Pep Guardiola's direction was a prospect that the whole soccer world was looking forward to. Pep had secured 14 out of 19 possible titles during his tenure with FC Barcelona before taking a year off, and Bayern had just taken the treble under former coach Jupp Heynckes with a style based predominantly on going forward quickly with the ball. Guardiola's style of soccer, on the other hand, is better described as control and possession.

OFFENSIVE

Pep prefers to control the game, which means possessing the ball as much as possible. His style has often been referred to as tiki taka, but Pep actually prefers to have possession with a purpose. The way in which Bayern attack would now be accomplished with positional play. In other words, all Bayern players would have to learn and follow certain rules when in possession of the ball. The picture on the left demonstrates the lines that Pep has put on the field during practice. You can see that there are both horizontal and vertical lines all over the field of play. No matter who is on the field for Bayern, each player now has specific tasks when in possession. This field setup allows the players to become aware of their tasks when in certain positions. The movement of the ball, the movement and position of the opponent, and the movement and position of other Bayern players will determine their decision making. The ball becomes the focal point; wherever the ball is on the field, the player will now recognize the optimal position that he should be in. In other words, the player must recognize the position he needs to be in at all times and be ready to adapt to where the ball is on the field. A fundamental aspect of Pep's strategy of possession is that his players ideally need to use around fifteen shorter or longer distance passes in an effort to break down the opposition. These fifteen passes allow Bayern to shape the opposing team as they attempt to break them down. For example, when Bayern wins the ball and has clear possession, they identify that they are going to try and isolate Costa in a 1-v-1 against the opposing outside back on the left side of the field. Bayern uses around twelve passes to transition the opposing team to the right side of the field. After these twelve passes, Bayern then use their next passes to switch the ball back to the left for Costa to attack the outside back in a 1-v-1 situation.

Pep is known for utilizing different systems of play from game to game and he is not afraid to change the system within a game. Changing to different systems allows Pep to determine how the other team can adjust. He also has the unique method of focusing on the individual strengths of each player and adapting their position. This means that a player for Pep is not playing where he has played in the past, but that he is playing where his individual strengths can be utilized as best as possible for the system. For example, the role for the majority of left backs is to support their winger, provide width, and overlap. In the case of David Alaba for Bayern, Pep gives Alaba the go-ahead to underlap the winger instead, due to his specific strength of combining effectively, even when in the middle of the field in the midst of heavy pressure. In addition, Alaba possesses amazing finishing ability both inside and outside the box. Philipp Lahm is another great example of this. Lahm, traditionally a right back when Bayern is not in possession of the ball, will transition to a holding midfield player when Bayern regains possession.

Initially, the way Bayern played under Pep in his first year was a bit of a concern for the die-hard German soccer fans as they were concerned that the Bayern way of attack was too slow and too centered on keeping the ball instead of going at the other teams. It is well-known that Germans prefer a more direct (and efficient) way of doing things! However, Guardiola brought in players well-known for their excellent speed and dribbling capabilities, like Douglas Costa and Kingsley Coman, to match his system to the style of the Bundesliga. These types of players provide Bayern with a variety of ways to attack other than combining through teams. They now have the option of simply giving the ball to players on the wing. This option gives the wingers a chance to beat their opponent in a 1-v-1 battle and deliver into the box.

In conclusion, watching Bayern attack is a highly enjoyable experience. This is the case because you never know which players will play in which system and what each player's individual roles will be within that system.

DEFENSIVE

As was mentioned in the offensive section, Guardiola prefers to have control and this is also seen in his defensive tactics. Many teams have a reactive way of defending and adjusting to what the opposition does with the ball. Bayern, to the contrary, has already prepared for defending by the manner in which they are attacking. The Bayern players attack in triangles and diamonds, making it extremely difficult for the opposition to beat multiple Bayern players with just one pass if they take possession. The moment Bayern loses the ball, they immediately counter press the opposition. The key to successful counter-pressing is that the team is prepared to win the ball back before they even lose possession of the ball. Teams that are skilled in counter-pressing are teams that attack with many of the players in close proximity to the ball carrier. In other words, even if they lose possession, they already have plenty of players around to pressure the opposing player with the ball and to effectively cut off his immediate passing options.

An interesting aspect of Bayern's counter-pressing strategy is that even if the opponent is able to release pressure, either by passing the ball backwards or even to the goalkeeper, Bayern will push multiple players up the field to continue pressing. This greatly reduces the opposing team's ability to build up from the back. Again, we see how this strategy provides Bayern with the greatest control as they make the decisions in the game, even when not in possession of the ball.

Because Bayern plays such a risky defensive strategy by leaving space behind their defense, they need goalkeeper Manuel Neuer to play almost as a sweeper-keeper because most teams attempt to beat Bayern on the counter-attack with long balls. Another key to Bayern's effective defensive strategy is a player such as Jerome Boateng, a center back and top athlete. He wins many of the long balls played by the opposing team by clearing the ball with a header or beating the opponent through sheer speed. When the opposing team is able to break down Bayern's press, they usually set up on the edge of their own box in a 4-1-4-1 shape, trying to keep the distance between the lines as compact as possible.

To summarize Bayern's strategy of defense, they use preventative measures such as good positioning to defend while attacking. However, this system does have the risk of leaving a lot of space in behind the defense by playing with a high line.

CASE STUDY #1:
A BAYERN MUNICH WIN

January 22, 2016

Player Lineups for Hamburg (white) vs. FC Bayern Munich (red) (with player tendencies)

Hamburg vs. Bayern

1:2

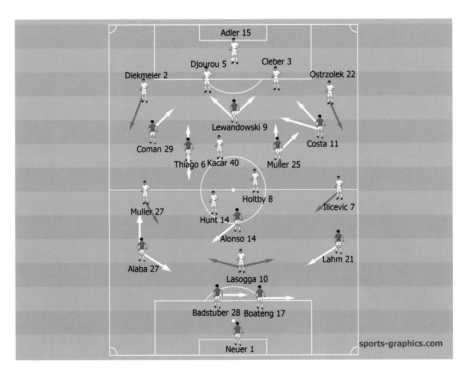

36 SECONDS

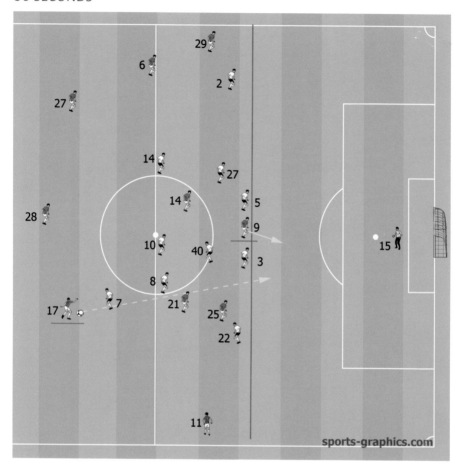

sports-graphics.com

In the beginning of the game, Hamburg attempts to make the field more compact horizontally and vertically. By doing so, they leave a huge space in behind their back four in order to stay connected to their midfield. Pep has his team set up to take whatever their opponent gives them. In this instance, Hamburg gives them the space in behind. Jerome Boateng is not afraid to play the long ball in behind to connect with Robert Lewandowski. Bayern is able to recognize this in only 36 seconds, indicating that if Hamburg persists with the high line, Bayern will go in behind with the speed of Costa, Coman, and Lewandowski.

19 MINUTES, 58 SECONDS

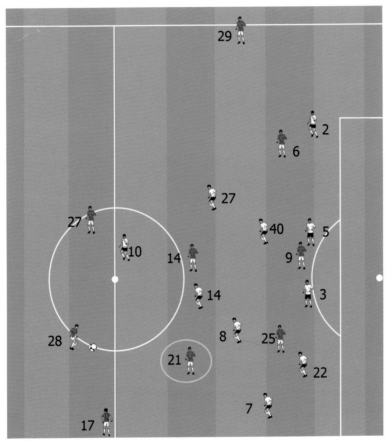

Now we are looking at Bayern's setup when in controlled possession of the field. Bayern have been unable to break Hamburg on the counter and Hamburg adjusts to reduce the space in behind their back four. The setup for Bayern is a 1-3-2-4-1 where Lahm (yellow circle) moves from his right back position to join Xabi Alonso in the right holding midfielder position. As you can see, Costa and Coman provide the width to the Bayern team; Thiago and Müller are occupying the half spaces between the Hamburg back four and midfield four; and Lewandowski is in a true number 9 position between the two center backs. Here you can see Guardiola's use of positional play and the organization of his team when in possession of the ball. Bayern creates many triangles and diamonds by never having more than three players on any horizontal line at the same time, and never having more than two players on the same vertical line.

7 MINUTES, 59 SECONDS

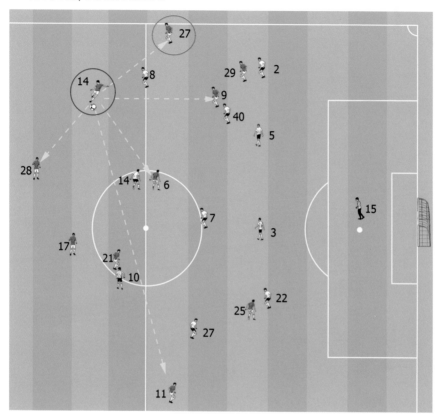

In this buildup from the back, Bayern creates different options to break down Hamburg's lines by the off-ball movement. Costa is providing width on the right side and Müller is ready for a diagonal ball in behind Hamburg's back four. On the side of the ball Coman (left winger) comes inside, taking Hamburg's right back with him and creating space for Alaba (left back, red circle) to push up higher. He then becomes the player responsible for giving the width on that side for Bayern. Alaba's higher and wider position creates space on the left side because Hamburg's right winger is forced to drop deep with him. Xabi Alonso (blue circle) can now drift in to the newly created space by the movement from Coman and Alaba to receive the ball there. This is one of the best positions for Alonso to receive the ball as he can now play the long diagonal ball with his strong foot to multiple Bayern players behind Hamburg's first line of pressure. One of the players he can find is Lahm, who transitions from his right back position to the holding midfielder position.

30 MINUTES, 23 SECONDS

Pep does not like to waste a sequence of ball possession in the buildup of play, which means if there are no options to go forward, Bayern will be content to possess the ball, even if they have to go backwards. In this frame, Hamburg does a great job pressing Bayern high up the field either by marking tightly (on Lahm) or putting Bayern players in their defensive shadows and blocking the passing lanes (to Alonso and Alaba). Bayern is unable to build up through Lahm or Alonso, the preferred duo in starting an attack. However, Boateng has no problem in starting the attack from scratch by passing it back to Neuer, one of the best goalkeepers around with the ball at his feet.

23 MINUTES, 17 SECONDS

When Bayern moves down the line to cross the ball, multiple players are in the box doing one of two things: setting up to win the second ball, or pressing immediately if Hamburg wins the second ball. Coman breaks through on the left side with David Alaba making an underlapping run from his left back position. At the same time, Thomas Müller comes from his midfield number 10 position, and Lewandowski arrives in the box. Müller and Lewandowski are both holding their runs, creating space for themselves because Hamburg's back four are dropping with the ball. This enables them to attack the space they have given themselves for when the cross arrives. Simultaneously, Lahm and Thiago position themselves in a manner so that they can immediately press any of Hamburg's four midfielders should Hamburg win the second ball. Finally, on the far right, Costa comes into the space at the top of the box to win the second ball and have a shot himself.

22 MINUTES, 6 SECONDS

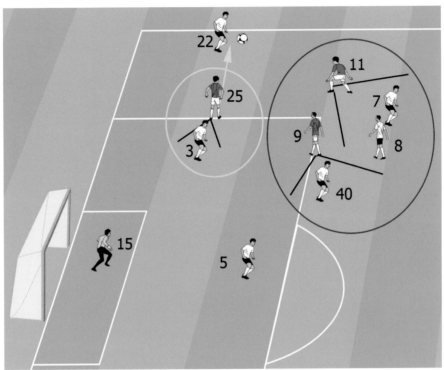

During transitions, Bayern Munich plays a highly aggressive counter pressing game. This can be seen almost immediately after they lose the ball. The closest player (Müller) presses the Hamburg player on the ball while at the same time placing Hamburg's center back in his defensive shadow, effectively taking him out of the game. The other Bayern players do not just mark the closest passing options, but they also position themselves in front of their man to put these players in their defensive shadows as well. All Bayern players in the back must be prepared for the long ball, and with players like Boateng and Badstuber, they win the majority of them. The Hamburg player currently in possession has no time on the ball due to the pressure on his short passing options. If he chooses to pass long, he knows that Bayern's center backs will most likely win those aerial duels.

9 MINUTES, 21 SECONDS

If Hamburg were able to release the ball out of Bayern's counter-pressing game (here Hamburg's center back looks to pass it back to his goalkeeper), Bayern would continue to press to dictate the game, even when not in possession of the ball. As you can see here, all of the outlets for Hamburg's center back are marked, so he is forced to play the ball back to his goalkeeper in an effort to maintain possession. Another option would have been to play the long ball, but as seen previously, it is highly likely that Bayern's defenders would win the aerial ball. As soon as the Hamburg player passes back to the keeper, Bayern continues to press and closes down potential options for the Hamburg keeper to build up the play, again forcing him to go long.

35 MINUTES, 31 SECONDS

In this picture, you can see Bayern's setup when forced to defend deep after being unsuccessful in regaining possession after pressing or counter-pressing. The shape that Bayern prefers in these situations is a 1-4-1-4-1. Lahm (yellow circle) will return to the back four while Xabi Alonso (blue circle) plays the number 6 role, and Lewandowski operates as the lone striker. Bayern's back four and midfield four stay connected and attempt to limit the space between these lines as much as possible. Additionally, the spaces between each player within these two lines is decent, although Badstuber and Thiago (red circles) could both push in just a little more to ball-side. If Hamburg's center midfielders begin to make runs inside the box, Xabi will then join the back four to temporarily create a back five. Lewandowski's role as the lone striker is to anticipate the counter-attack by either finding space behind Hamburg's high outside backs or possessing the ball to begin Bayern's transition.

CASE STUDY #2: BEATING BAYERN MUNICH

December 5, 2015

Player Lineups for Borussia Mönchengladbach (white) vs. FC Bayern Munich (red) (with player tendencies)

Mönchengladbach vs. Bayern

3:1

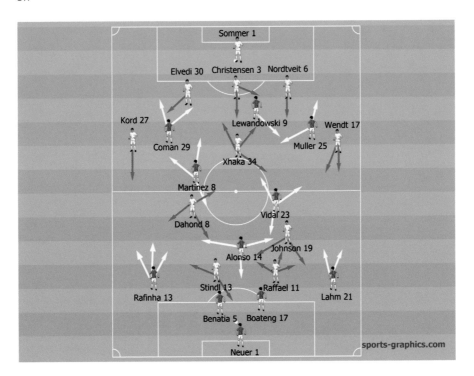

5 MINUTES, 21 SECONDS

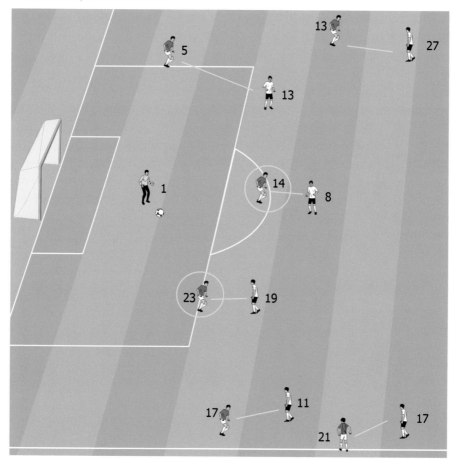

M. Gladbach's plan of attack against Bayern Munich is immediately evident in the opening minutes of the game. Their setup is a 1-5-3-2/1-3-5-2 in which every M. Gladbach player man marks a Bayern player when Bayern has the ball in their defensive third. The three M. Gladbach center backs mark the three Bayern forwards, the three M. Gladbach center midfielders mark Bayern's three center midfielders, the wing backs mark Bayern's outside backs, and the two forwards mark Bayern's center backs. Bayern is accustomed to teams defending against them in a 4-4-2 shape with the center backs being marked, so to keep their passing game working, Bayern moves one of their central midfielders between their two center backs to help start the attack. However, M. Gladbach's strategy of defending makes it basically impossible for Bayern to build up from the back. This can be seen in the picture; the two Bayern center backs are very wide, so two center midfielders are coming back to start the buildup. However, M. Gladbach players follow them all the way and Neuer does not know where to play the ball.

8 MINUTES, 32 SECONDS

In this picture, you can see how M. Gladbach sets up when defending deep. When the ball is in the middle, there are three center midfielders that are in front of their back five as well as two forwards playing centrally. This forces Bayern to play to the wing where M. Gladbach can then pressure them hard and cut off all available passing lanes. The ball is played to Bayern's left back (Rafinha), and M. Gladbach's right wing back pressures him immediately. M. Gladbach's left wing back also tucks in to create a back four shape and the defense pushes over to ball-side. Simultaneously, two of M. Gladbach's center midfielders move toward the ball to reduce all of the space around it. The closest M. Gladbach forward moves back to place the Bayern player in his defensive shadow, reducing Bayern's backward option of switching the field.

22 MINUTES, 48 SECONDS

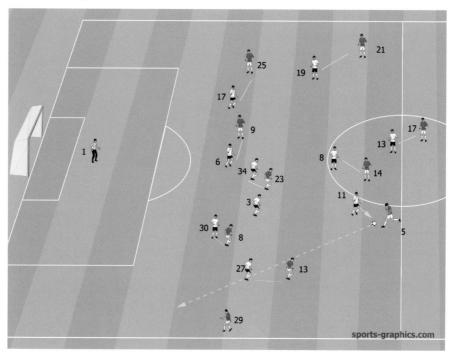

Bayern attempts to adjust to M. Gladbach's man-marking by trying to hit longer balls into space. In this picture, the ball is in the middle of the field and M. Gladbach has tightly marked all of Bayern's short options. A M. Gladbach player continuously puts pressure on the ball carrier, so the Bayern player now tries to play into the space left open by the right wing back rather than building up play like they usually do. By playing in this manner, M. Gladbach takes away what Bayern has been known to do since Pep took over: offensive and defensive control. This control involves proactivity in all situations of the game. However, M. Gladbach found a way to control the game by setting up in a way that forces Bayern to play the ball where M. Gladbach wanted it.

22 MINUTES, 25 SECONDS

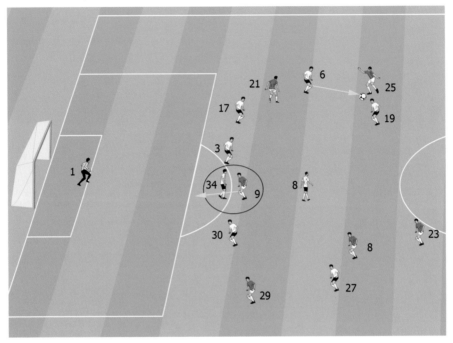

When Bayern makes it into the final third, M. Gladbach's main priority is a back four setup to limit Bayern's combination options or to play through them. Keeping a back four setup is a priority, even if it means giving up their man-marking system at this juncture.

Bayern's right forward, Müller, drops into the half space. He is quickly followed by M. Gladbach's center back in an attempt to reduce Müller's space of operating in such a critical area of the field. What happens next is quite difficult to accomplish; however M. Gladbach's Xhaka is certainly one of the smartest players in the Bundesliga. When Xhaka sees that a hole has opened up between the right center back and right wing back, he drops quickly in that space to keep the distance between the defenders as small as possible. This gives Lewandowski, who was making a run into that space, very little room to operate.

34 MINUTES, 32 SECONDS

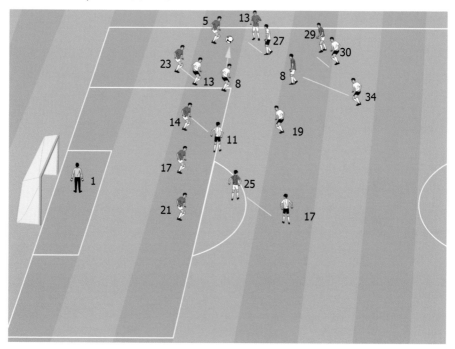

Bayern is accustomed to having many players around the ball in order to play through teams with their great short passing game and elite technical skills. Teams defending zonally often have a difficult time managing Bayern as they tend to overload specific zones.

This picture shows multiple Bayern players around the ball in an attempt to combine their way out of pressure. However, M. Gladbach's man-marking setup creates the opposite effect for Bayern; the more players Bayern bring close to the ball, the tighter the space becomes. When a Bayern player comes to support, they inadvertently bring an M. Gladbach marker with them. As a result, M. Gladbach is highly successful in winning the ball back from Bayern in transition.

In this picture, you can see that five Bayern players are within a 10-x-5-yard space, also bringing five M. Gladbach players with them. You can also clearly see the difference of positioning between M. Gladbach's pressing game and Bayern's. When covering the outlets, M. Gladbach players are behind the players, not in front (as Bayern typically does) because they are aware of Bayern's terrific movement and speed off of the ball.

34 MINUTES, 53 SECONDS

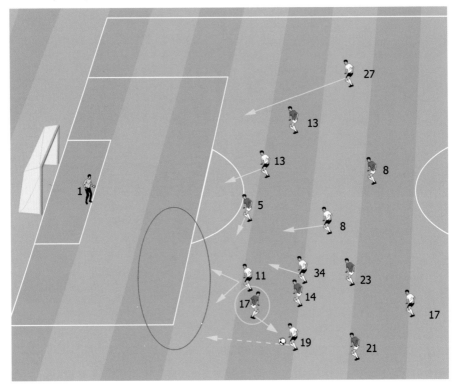

One of the hallmarks of Bayern's playing style is a defensively aggressive response when they lose possession. When Bayern loses possession, the next closest Bayern player steps up to press the opponent in possession, while the other Bayern players shift over to cover the next closest player. This picture demonstrates the many holes that were created from this defensive strategy which provided M. Gladbach with a scoring opportunity.

In this picture, you can see that Bayern's right back, Philipp Lahm, has lost possession. Boateng (Bayern center back) now becomes the closest player to the ball. He steps to put pressure on M. Gladbach's player, but this leaves space in behind him. The differences between M. Gladbach's strategy of defending (man-marking) and Bayern's strategy of defending (next man steps to put pressure on) are actually of great benefit for M. Gladbach's offensive transition game. M. Gladbach is able to exploit Bayern's defense because they have many players forward when defending. As soon as M. Gladbach wins the ball and Bayern steps to press, M. Gladbach exploits the spaces left open.

MANCHESTER CITY FC

HISTORY

The formation of Manchester City Football Club began in 1880 and was founded by two reverends in Gorton, Manchester. The original name was St. Mark's but seven years later, the club changed locations and became Ardwick AFC.[31] They finally became Manchester City in 1894 to represent the entire city. Manchester City had the honor of playing the first live televised Monday Night Football game in 1992, when the Premier League was formed. The club has been a mainstay of the Premier league since 2002, even after a rough period of promotion and relegation. In 2008, the Abu Dhabi United Group purchased the club and invested the money necessary to bring in quality players and coaches to compete in one of the best leagues in the world. The 2011-2012 season saw their first Premier League title and current coach, Manuel Pellegrini, doubled the tally with another title in the 2013-2014 season. Manchester City's most successful run as a team has occurred with the current squad, winning a total of five major titles over the past six seasons.

Manchester City currently plays at the Etihad Stadium, located on a massive facility that houses not only the stadium but also a state-of-the-art youth academy and an incredible fan zone complex. The stadium holds 48,000 fans and approximately 10 million fans have passed through the gates over the last ten years.

Team Motto: *Pride in Battle.*

---

31   *See Wikipedia.*

HONORS

- ★ First Division/Premier League: 4
- ★ Second Division: 7
- ★ Third Division 1
- ★ FA Cup: 5
- ★ League Cup: 3
- ★ Community Shield: 4
- ★ UEFA Cup Winner's Cup: 1

MANCHESTER CITY COACHES

ROBERTO MANCINI (2009-2013)

Fifty-one-year-old Roberto Mancini took the helm at Manchester City for the 2009-2013 seasons, having started his managerial career in his native Italy with spells at Fiorentina, Lazio, and Internazionale. Mancini was a highly accomplished attacking midfield player himself before transitioning into management. He played over 400 times for the Serie "A" side Sampdoria but also had spells at Lazio, Bologna, and England's Leicester City. He represented his country 36 times, but could not hold down a regular starting spot.

There can be no doubt that Mancini's guidance jump started Manchester City's journey toward becoming a major club again. It was during Mancini's tenure that influential players such as David Silva, Yaya Touré, and Sergio Agüero signed for Manchester City. When he first arrived at Manchester City, Mancini was viewed as what one might call a typical Italian coach: having high tactical knowledge and implementing a strong defensive organization.

After a good start at Manchester City during his first couple of seasons using those principles, Mancini signed some more offensive-minded players, such as David Silva, Yaya Touré, and Sergio Agüero. With this group, Mancini was able to play an increasingly offensive style of soccer as he continued at Manchester City.

During the 2011-2012 season, Mancini typically set up his team in a 4-2-2-2 system due to the numerous incredible forwards at his disposal such as Tevez and Agüero as well as Dzeko and Balotelli. He used Silva and Nasri as inverted wingers, meaning they would drift from their wide positions into the half spaces and central zone, creating space for Manchester City's offensive outside backs to join the attack and provide width. To keep a solid defensive structure, Mancini typically played with two holding midfielders, usually Yaya Touré and Gareth Barry.

With this attacking brand of soccer, Mancini also placed a higher focus on possession. Defensively, Mancini would use a 4-4-2 shape; the two inverted wingers would join the two holding midfielders. Mancini also used a higher pressing game due to the defensive hard work of Agüero and Tevez.

The 2011-2012 season brought Manchester City the league title in a dramatic fashion. It wasn't until Agüero scored a late winning strike at home versus Queens Park Rangers on the last day of the season that they sealed the title over their bitter rivals, Manchester United.

However, a lack of success in the Champions League and an FA Cup final loss to relegation stricken Wigan Athletic signaled the beginning of the end for the Italian at the Etihad.

HONORS AT MANCHESTER CITY
- ★ Premier League: 1
- ★ FA Cup: 1
- ★ Community Shield: 1

MANUEL PELLEGRINI (2013-2016)

The 62-year-old Chilean arrived at the Etihad following a very successful coaching spell with Malaga CF. Manuel Pellegrini was a one-club man as a player, making over 450 appearances as a center back for Universidad de Chile. He also represented his country 28 times during his career.

Pellegrini managed a variety of clubs in South America for fifteen years before arriving in Europe in 2004 to take charge of Villarreal. He achieved unprecedented success at this relatively small club, leading them to Champions League qualification in his first season and then a place in the semifinal of the same competition the following year.

His success at Villarreal did not go unnoticed, and he was soon appointed as manager of soccer giants, Real Madrid. However, his stay at the Bernabeu was short-lived and he was sacked after just one season at the helm.

From there, Pellegrini was appointed at Malaga CF and once again took a smaller club to heights never seen before. Malaga CF experienced their first qualification to the Champions League under Pellegrini's guidance. While there, Malaga CF made a heroic run to the quarterfinal before a dramatic loss to German side Borussia Dortmund.

In 2013, Pellegrini left Malaga to take over at Manchester City. He has enjoyed a relatively successful period in charge at the Etihad. Perhaps the highlight of his tenure thus far was winning the Premier League title, coming from behind to take it from Liverpool at the tail end of the season.

HONORS AT MANCHESTER CITY

★   Premier League: 1
★   League Cup: 2

MANCHESTER CITY FC KEY PLAYERS

JOE HART (2006-PRESENT)

Joe Hart, with his intimidating height of 6'5", has firmly established himself as the undisputed number one goalkeeper for both Manchester City and England. He has been at Manchester City for almost a decade and was a key part in the transition of the club from an average team to a team that is now a perennial title contender. Hart has won the Premier League twice as the starting goalkeeper.

Hart is without a doubt one of the most intense and confident goalkeepers in the game today and keeps his defenders on their toes with his constant communication. The Englishman is a consistently solid shot stopper and effectively commands his box without fear by navigating traffic to punch away those clearly dangerous balls to the box.

Hart has been the starting goalkeeper under both Mancini and Pellegrini, but he has also had spells of temporary relegation to the reserve role under both coaches. Despite being dropped, he has always managed to return to the starting position.

Hart has experienced the rewards of the tactical adjustments that both Mancini and Pellegrini made to the defensive side of Manchester City's game. After Mancini arrived, Manchester City improved their defensive organization, especially during his first couple of years. Mancini kept many players back defensively to err on the side of caution, a massive bonus for a young goalkeeper as Hart was at the time. Under Pellegrini, Manchester City tend to hold their defensive line on the edge of the penalty box as long as possible, a tactic that greatly benefits Hart. This reduces the heavy traffic in front of Hart, making it easier for him to come out for crosses as there is a lower likelihood that he will run into the opposition or even his own players. Furthermore, it makes it easier for Hart to organize his back four.

Manchester City is a strong financial powerhouse, perhaps one of the strongest that exists in modern-day soccer. However, there has not been a conscious effort to replace

Joe Hart, indicating just what his worth is to the club as well as the trust that the team and manager place in him.

VINCENT KOMPANY (2008-PRESENT)

The physically imposing 6'4" Vincent Kompany has established a reputation over a long career as one of the best center halves in world soccer. Still only 29 years old, Kompany started his career as a wunderkind in his native Belgium, making his Anderlecht debut at just 17 years old.[32] He won Belgian Player of the Year just one season later, quickly becoming one of the most sought after young talents in Europe. Kompany joined the German side Hamburg in 2006, experiencing a surprisingly difficult couple of seasons before signing at Manchester City in 2008. This was the moment where his career truly flourished.

Kompany is the prototypical modern defender. He combines significant physicality, strength, and athleticism with above-average technical ability for his position. Kompany is also a competent reader of the game, evidenced by decisions to step out of the back four and placing pressure on a midfielder or a forward who dropped back into midfield, which is perhaps one of the most tactically difficult decisions a modern center back must make. These skills have led to consistent starting appearances as the center back under both Mancini and Pellegrini.

Kompany's tactical and technical skills have made him the perfect fit for Manchester City's center back position, a role he has consistently played. Under Mancini, Kompany's defensive abilities were much more apparent in the box as well as his adeptness in defending deeper. It was more common for Manchester City to have less possession during Mancini's first two seasons; however this enabled Kompany to consistently demonstrate his defensive prowess.

In Manchester City's first championship season under Mancini, they began to play a more offensively focused game. During this time, it was evident that Kompany was self-assured when in possession of the ball and that he also made great decisions off of the ball. The domination of possession and playing out of the back only increased with Pellegrini's arrival.

---

32   See Wikipedia.

The significant tactical change made in Pellegrini's system that had a direct influence on Kompany was defending outside the box, indicating the massive trust his coach had in Kompany's speed and tactical awareness. As the center back, Kompany is responsible for deciding whether to keep the defensive line high or to mark the forward. It is no easy feat to make these types of decisions at the highest level of soccer and against some of the best forwards in the world.

One of Kompany's better attributes (which is often overlooked) is his technical skill when in possession. This is integral when playing for a top team who will attempt to have the majority of possession, while other teams tend to defend deep in their half. He is one of an elite group of center backs in world soccer, especially when it comes to dribbling out of the back, forcing the opposition to put pressure on him. This opens up his teammates to become passing options.

Kompany is widely regarded as one of the greatest leaders in soccer—he is the captain of both Manchester City and Belgium. The degree of influence he has for both teams is evident, which is highlighted when he is absent.

ALEKSANDER KOLAROV (2010-PRESENT)

Aleksander Kolarov, the Serbian powerhouse, joined Manchester City in July of 2010. Mancini brought Kolarov to Manchester City after a string of superb performances for Italian giants, Lazio. Kolarov is one of the most physically imposing left backs in the world, standing at an intimidating 6'2". Despite his impressive physical stature and his position as left back, Kolarov is perhaps better known for his offensive talents.

Kolarov possesses an absolute cannon for a left foot and is not afraid to test the goalkeepers from distances considered out of range for most players. Kolarov is equally adept at using his left foot as a creative tool and is a dangerous crosser from open play, either from the offensive half spaces or using the length of the field to fire in crosses for the forwards and deeper midfielders to score.

His left foot is a massive asset at set pieces such as corner kicks or free kicks, especially from wide positions. His set piece ability is not limited to crosses; he also possesses the rare skill of taking direct free kicks from close range, bending them over the wall.

Last but certainly not least is his massive threat to score on set pieces from further distances.

It is evident how proficient Kolarov is with set pieces; no matter whom Manchester City has acquired in the past six years (managers or players), Kolarov remains consistent with set pieces, regardless of the players on the field at the time.

With such brilliant offensive ability, Kolarov is perfect for the tactical setup under both Mancini and Pellegrini. Both managers preferred to push the outside backs high up the field when building out of the back, and then using Kolarov as the main provider of width for the team. This is evident when Kolarov plays in the left back position; he will push up the field consistently to be level with the opposing outside back. From time to time, Kolarov has been used as a left midfielder, but this is a fairly uncommon occurrence.

YAYA TOURÉ (2010-PRESENT)

Roberto Mancini signed Yaya Touré in July 2010 from FC Barcelona. An interesting fact about Touré is that his brother, Kolo Touré, played three seasons with him for Manchester City before moving to Liverpool. Yaya won the African Footballer of the Year award for four consecutive seasons (2011-2014) and was a part of the Premier League Team of the Year following the 2011 and 2013 seasons. [33]

Yaya Touré played a holding role for Barcelona, a position that Mancini changed almost immediately when Yaya arrived in Manchester. Mancini wanted to use Yaya's rare talents more extensively in both an offensive and defensive capacity. Under Mancini, Yaya continued to play mainly in the holding midfield role, but now had a license to join the attack in a supporting role.

Since Pellegini took over, Yaya plays in multiple positions in Manchester City's midfield, depending on availability of other players and the type of opponent. Yaya has even occasionally played a pure holding midfield role. Under Pellegrini, Yaya usually plays as the box-to-box midfielder, much like a number 8; in other words, Yaya helps out in a defensive shape, but goes full speed when attacking in order to assist the forwards.

---

33   Ibid.

Yaya also plays in a lot of the games as an offensive midfielder, much like a number 10. When playing in the number 10 role he has a lot more freedom offensively and less responsibility defensively.

Yaya is one of the most natural athletically gifted players of his generation. He is capable of effortlessly covering large quantities of the pitch. Yaya is also blessed with a brilliant right foot capable of scoring and creating goals. When running with the ball at his feet, the Ivorian international is immensely difficult to stop due to his combination of brute strength and technical ability. Yaya is also a top quality set piece aficionado and is a genuine threat from any position on the field, within 35 yards of goal.

KEVIN DE BRUYNE (2015-PRESENT)

The 5'11" Kevin De Bruyne has many skills, one of which is speaking three languages: English, French, and Dutch. After an incredible 2014-2015 season with Wolfsburg, De Bruyne was named Footballer of the Year in Germany, catching the attention of Manchester City. Pellegrini signed De Bruyne the following summer (2015) and De Bruyne immediately became one of the most indispensable players in the current Manchester City squad. Belgian international De Bruyne is perhaps one of the most dynamic offensive threats in the world. Predominantly a playmaker, De Bruyne also presents a constant threat to score as well, separating him from many of the other top playmakers around.

Pellegrini typically uses De Bruyne on the right offensive side, using him to drift in to the middle of the field when their outside back provides the width. While in this formation, De Bruyne will play more of a central attacking role, typically the Belgian's preferred position. When Agüero, Silva, Touré, and De Bruyne are all healthy and playing together, they usually overload the right side, either as small groups or all together. The devastating qualities of these players in tight spaces and their ability to hold the ball under pressure or combine together make Manchester City's right offensive side one of the most dangerous in the world.

It is for this reason that many teams in the Premier League and the Champions League experience extreme difficulties in managing Manchester City's offensive prowess, especially in the right area of the field.

As previously mentioned, De Bruyne's instinct for goals truly separates him from the majority of midfield operators. He is equally adept at close-range finishes as he is with long-range efforts. De Bruyne possesses phenomenal technical ability and has brilliant composure on the ball. He is a deceptively fast player who can operate effectively on the wing as well as the middle of the field (his preferred position.) As one would expect given his elite technical ability, De Bruyne also excels at set piece deliveries.

Many consider De Bruyne to be integral in the attacking play of the Belgian national team; high praise considering the elite players he is surrounded with. De Bruyne is quite simply a chance-creating machine. Perhaps there are not many better than he in this regard.

DAVID SILVA (2014-PRESENT)

David Silva, another integral player for Manchester City, was a key member of the Spanish National Team that won three consecutive international tournaments (Euro 2008, World Cup 2010, Euro 2012). In 2011, Silva also made the Premier League Team of the Year. It is rare for Silva to not be a part of a highly successful team. The Spaniard is usually a key reason for the accomplishments of the squads he has been involved with.

Left-footed Silva is a magical playmaker with the ball at his feet, proving time and time again that he is capable of unlocking even the most airtight defensive units in the world. This can largely be credited to his high levels of elusiveness and technical ability. Silva is no doubt effective, playing as a number 10 or by cutting in from either wing. Both Mancini and Pellegrini have used Silva in all three of these positions. No matter where Silva starts, he tends to end up drifting into the two offensive half spaces, receiving the ball between the defensive and midfield lines and giving himself the ability to dribble at the opposition or to combine, play the killer pass, or finish with a shot himself.

Under Mancini, Silva was mainly used as the left winger, drifting inside or in the number 10 position (offensive central midfielder). Currently, under Pellegrini, Silva operates mainly as the number 10 (offensive central midfielder) or as the right winger drifting inside. The makeup of Pellegrini's side is to overload the right side. When this occurs, Silva will start wide but then drift inside, and the outside back will provide width at that time. Another scenario will see Silva starting as the central midfielder but then drifting to the right side to overload and combine through the right channel.

While on the left wing, Silva will sometimes drift into the half space because his tendency and preference is to be near the ball. Silva will often attempt to create space for Sterling on the left side by staying away from the left side, waiting for Sterling to break through to the end line. At this point, Sterling can cross the ball back to the top of the box or across the opposing teams box where Silva is ready to pounce, especially given his precise ability to finish in that area of the field.

Silva's primary strength is his low center of gravity, allowing him to maneuver in and out of tight situations while in possession of the ball. He also has unbelievable composure in these situations, allowing him to play the decisive pass at the most lethal time.

While not a prolific goal threat, he has frequently proven his capability of scoring key goals in the big games. Silva is the definition of a big game player.

SERGIO AGÜERO (2011-PRESENT)

The 5'8" Argentina native was destined to be a top class soccer player. His debut for Independiente occurred when he was just 15 years old. Atletico Madrid was the team to woo him to Europe at the age of 18, and Agüero demonstrated immediate readiness to adapt to his new surroundings by scoring a goal every two games for the Spanish giants. It was only a matter of time before he made another big move. Manchester City sealed his services for 45 million euros in July 2011. His time at the Etihad has only further enhanced his reputation as one of the top strikers in the world.

During the 2011-2012 season, Mancini preferred to play with one striker but a dilemma was presented with possessing so many top-class forwards. With Agüero, Tevez, Balotelli, and Dzeko, Mancini altered his system just several games into the season, now playing with two strikers where one has consistently been Agüero.

The tactical lineup of Mancini was a match made in heaven for a player with Agüero's strengths. Defensively, Agüero is known for his work ethic, a perfect fit for Mancini's pressing and counter-pressing system. Offensively, Mancini adapted the possession system during the 2011-2012 season, another good match for Agüero's technical precision. Agüero is an incredibly technically and tactically adept player, making great decisions in determining when to come back to midfield to receive the ball in between the lines or in the half spaces.

The tactical point of view under Pellegrini has Manchester City playing more of a 4-2-3-1 system in the 2015-2016 season, making Agüero the lone striker. Manchester City plays a higher degree of attacking soccer, meaning more teams must defend deeper in games against them. This highlights Agüero's extraordinary movements in and around the opposing box.

Very few strikers possess similarly brilliant decision-making abilities about whether or not to stand still when the opposing defenders are dropping or when the defenders are standing and marking him to just make one quick move to gain the extra yard at the right moment. This extra yard is all that is needed due to Agüero's unbelievable finishing skills.

Agüero is one of those strikers that every coach would love to have on his team. No matter the opponent or outcome of the games, Agüero is still able to score goals due to his incredible individual talent.

Agüero is considered by many to be the best striker in the English Premier League. This point is difficult to argue because of his goal ratio and ability to perform in the biggest fixtures. Agüero also has a top-quality goal to game ratio with the Argentinian national team (32 goals in 69 games).

GENERAL SETUP UNDER MANUEL PELLEGRINI

OFFENSIVE

During the 2015-2016 season, Manchester City primarily used a 4-2-3-1 attacking shape. Pellegrini prefers to control the game through possession of the ball, but Manchester City will also stretch the opposing defense by going long when needed. The opposing team is now forced to make a decision: either stay compact on top of their own box to give up the midfield, or stay compact higher up the field, leaving space for Agüero and Sterling to run into.

Pellegrini and his Manchester City team prefer to build up patiently through the thirds of the field, creating space for the elite attacking players in the offensive half spaces. The Pellegrini method of using the half space highly depends on the personnel he has available and their individual attributes.

When in possession, Manchester City will spread out their back four, sending the outside backs high while one or both wingers drift inside from the sides and the lone striker stretches the other team. When attacking through the right side of the field, Pellegrini typically uses De Bruyne as the right-side midfielder, Silva in center midfield, and Agüero as the high forward. All three of these players are very comfortable in possession, using their quick decision-making abilities when under serious pressure. Pellegrini makes use of these strengths by overloading the right half spaces with De Bruyne coming inside from his wing position; meanwhile Manchester City's wing back will provide the width. Simultaneously, Silva will drift into the right half space from the center midfield position and Agüero will push over to the right side.

Teams have a difficult time managing so many players and maintaining their defensive shape. This usually results in Silva taking the ball on his preferred left foot in the right half space, then able to either play a through ball or deliver a dangerous cross to create scoring opportunities for Manchester City.

When Manchester City is attempting to break through on the left side, Silva will still drift to the left half space from time to time. However, the main threat on the left side is Sterling as the left winger, with the goal of isolating Sterling for a 1-v-1 situation against the opposing right back.

Manchester City is able to achieve this by reducing the degree that Silva and Agüero will push over to the ball on the left side, keeping the opposing defenders away. Another way that Sterling is able to get into the left offensive half space is when Silva is able to switch the ball to the left half space after receiving it in the right offensive half space. Manchester City has an incredible offensive threat in Aleksander Kolarov as well, typically in the left outside back position. Manchester City will push their outside backs high in order to keep the width while the three offensive midfielders occupy the offensive half spaces. This forces the opposition to play with a narrower shape, giving Manchester City's outside backs space on their flanks.

When Kolarov is in the starting lineup, Manchester City tries to create space for him so he can make the most of his incredible left foot, one that is renowned for serving high quality crosses into the box. Manchester City scores many of their goals from converting Kolarov's crosses with headers. Another strategy to use Kolarov's amazing left foot is for him to dribble to the byline to force the opposing back four to drop deep. He then can see the space left open at the top of the box, and can play the ball back into that space, finding the likes of Yaya Touré or Silva, lethal finishers from those areas.

Despite possessing many amazingly skilled players, the most important aspect of Manchester City's attacking game is through the power and finishing ability of Yaya Touré and the speed and skill in tight spaces, movement in the box, and finishing ability of Sergio Agüero. Even on a bad day, Manchester City can still rely on those two to decide a match with just one moment of individual brilliance.

In conclusion, Manchester City is a high possession-oriented team with a rather slow buildup. Pellegrini found a way to best utilize the strengths and abilities of his players, one of the reasons they have been so successful over a long period of time despite a few adjustments in player personnel for certain games.

DEFENSIVE

As discussed in the offensive section, Pellegrini prefers to patiently build up, a strategy that also translates to his defensive tactics. Many of the current top teams tend to defend proactively, including Bayern Munich and Barcelona under Guardiola or Enrique who prefer to dictate what the opposition does with the ball.

Manchester City, on the other hand, focuses more on the individual makeup of the players and their strengths. Players such as Yaya Touré, for example, are not known for their pressing or counter-pressing game.

Depending on the opposing team and the available player personnel that Manchester City has available, they usually defend with either a 4-4-2 or 4-3-3 shape. The main emphasis on the defensive shape is that Manchester City will focus on keeping the central zones compact, especially the midfield line regardless of whether they use three or four midfielders. As a result, the other team is forced to try to break through on the flanks. When the ball is played to one side of the field, the responsibility of one of the forwards is to cut off the opponent's ability to switch the ball back to the other side while the other forward pressures the ball carrier. Simultaneously, the rest of the Manchester City team will transition to the side of the ball, forcing the opposition to make a mistake or to try and win the ball back.

Manchester City is known for holding a high defensive line, a commonality among top teams. The reason for this is the greater the compactness is between the lines, the more difficult it is for the opposition to find space and receive the ball in those areas.

In the 2015-2016 season, the Manchester City back four attempted to hold their defensive line at the 18-yard line as long as possible, not stepping in their own box unless the ball was actually behind the line. This strategy creates more efficient defensive organization, shrinking the space between the defense and midfield lines tremendously as the other team gets into Manchester City's final third. This can limit the opposing team's offensive strategy as it places enormous pressure on the opposing player with the ball; the closer he gets to Manchester City's goal, the fewer options he has as it now becomes increasingly difficult to combine or pass to a teammate between these lines.

Manchester City also held this defensive line as long as possible because it reduces the number of bodies in front of goalkeeper Joe Hart when the opposing team attempts to cross the ball in from the wide channel. Now Hart can just come out and collect the ball with his hands in the open space in front of him.

It has to be said that Manchester City's defensive unit looks far more intimidating when Vincent Kompany is in the starting lineup due to his phenomenal leadership skills and his ability to read the game effectively, allowing him to better position himself, or direct other players into the perfect spot.

In conclusion, Manchester City's defensive tactics under Pellegrini might not be the most modern or cutting edge, but it is Pellegrini's philosophy to play to the individual strengths of the players. It is evident that Manchester City is very organized defensively and not afraid to adjust their defensive shape, using a variety of players to better defend against the strengths of their opponent.

CASE STUDY #1: A MANCHESTER CITY WIN

February 24, 2016

Player Lineups for Manchester City (red) vs. Dynamo Kiev (white) (with player tendencies)

Manchester City vs. Dynamo Kiev

3:1

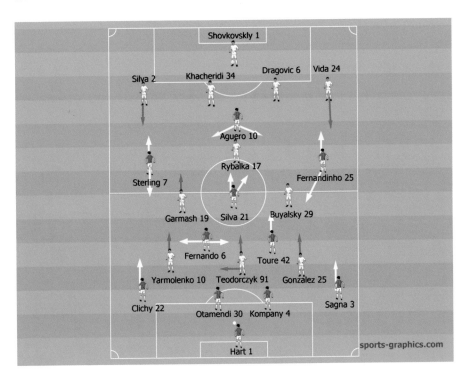

1 MINUTE, 53 SECONDS

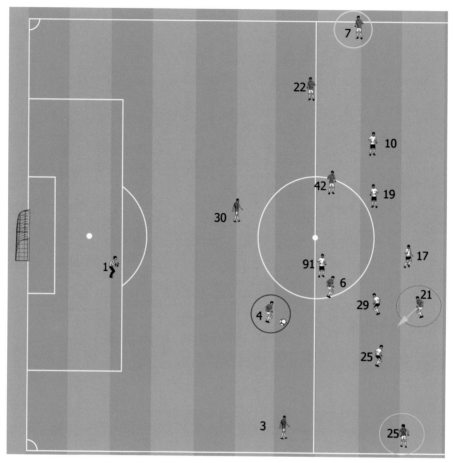

When Manchester City attacks, they are set up in a 1-4-2-3-1 shape, spreading their back four with two holding midfielders, three offensive midfielders, and one central forward who checks to the ball, or stretches the opposing back four.

The picture demonstrates how Manchester City builds up from the back. Dynamo Kiev is positioned in a 1-4-1-4-1 shape. The Manchester City back four are spread out and the Manchester City outside midfielders are now responsible for the width (Fernandinho on the right side, and Sterling on the left). Kompany, the central defender from Manchester City, carries the ball up the field, forcing a member of the opposition to pressure him. At the same time, Silva is checking to the ball in the right offensive half space behind the Dynamo Kiev midfield line.

36 MINUTES, 52 SECONDS

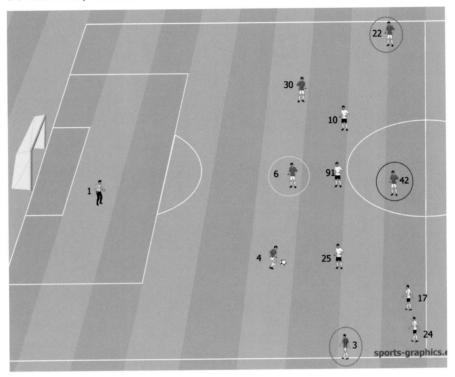

When the Manchester City center backs are pressed deeper in their own half, Fernando (6) comes in between the two center backs to help with the buildup or try and create more space for Yaya Touré (42), center of midfield. This is because one of Kiev's midfielders will follow Fernando. This picture shows that when Fernando drops in between the two center backs, Kiev brings up three forwards to press. As a result, Yaya Touré has a lot of free space to operate in. Manchester City's outside backs are also placed higher up the field, creating better passing angles and making it more difficult for Kiev to defend. Manchester City is now able to play around the first line of pressure by Kiev; their effective movements off the ball and the great passing angles created by the positioning of Manchester City's outside backs allow for this patient buildup.

38 MINUTES, 14 SECONDS

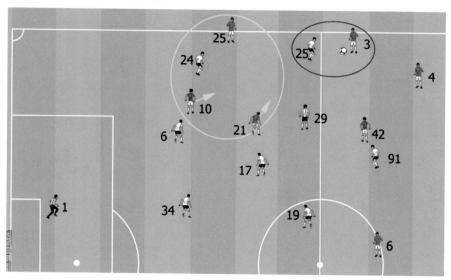

One of Manchester City's preferred methods of attack is to overload their right side and play with short passes and combination play through the other team. This strategy is so successful due to the great movements of Silva, who possesses impeccable timing of checking into the offensive right half space. He also possesses great dribbling technique, allowing him to combine with his strong left foot, even under extreme pressure from the opposition.

Here Manchester City creates a 3-v-1/3-v-2 situation between the defensive and midfield line of Dynamo Kiev. Manchester City's outside back Sagna dribbles up the field with the ball, forcing Kiev's left midfielder to pressure him in order to stop him from penetrating. This isolates Kiev's left back against Fernandinho (25), who is providing width for Manchester City on the left side. Meanwhile, Silva (21) drifts into this space from the center of the field along with forward Sergio Agüero (10). With these incredible technical players—who are adept in 1-v-1 situations—moving in, Kiev has a difficult time stopping the Manchester City attack.

39 MINUTES, 39 SECONDS

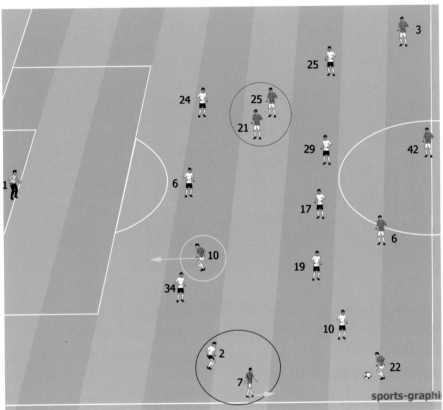

Manchester City's left-sided attacks are a different picture due to the unique skills that left forward, Sterling, provides. These skills include his extreme quickness and preference in taking on opponents in 1-v-1 situation.

This picture shows that as Manchester City's left back Clichy (22) builds the attack through the left side, Agüero (yellow circle) tries to stretch the defense by making a run in behind. Silva and Fernandinho stay away from the left side, helping Sterling create a 1-v-1 situation against Dynamo Kiev's right back. A 1-v-1 with Sterling on the ball tends to be a great opportunity for Manchester City. Sterling (blue circle) is creating space for himself by checking to the ball and positioning himself so it is played to his feet.

39 MINUTES, 41 SECONDS

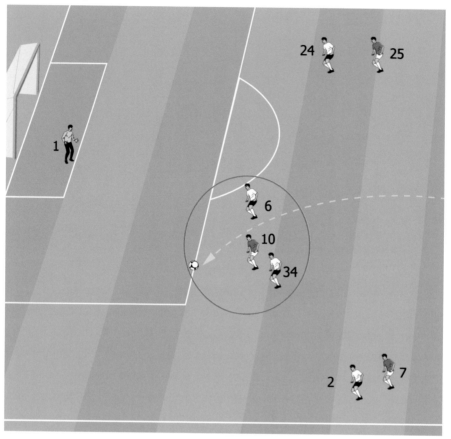

The name that comes to mind in a Manchester City style of attack is Sergio Agüero, currently one of the best strikers in the world. Pelligrini gives Agüero a lot of offensive freedom and Manchester City plays a more direct game than necessary due to the speed and amazing timing of Agüero's runs. This picture shows that as the Kiev right back steps to Sterling, it creates space behind him. Agüero recognizes this almost immediately and looks to exploit it with his speed, timing, and technical ability to control the long ball and attack the Kiev defense.

2 MINUTES, 3 SECONDS

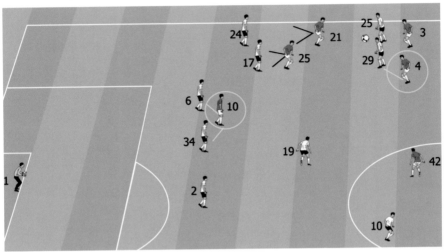

This picture shows Manchester City transitioning from attacking to defense on the right side of the field. Manchester City is aggressive at this point because after losing the ball on the right side, they still have multiple players on that side due to their tendency to attack by overloading the right side. When Manchester City loses the ball on the right side, they are able to win it back because of the sheer number of players around the ball. These players are aggressively pressing the moment the ball is lost. As a result, Dynamo Kiev is not able to spread out to create good passing options for themselves.

In this picture, Sagna loses the ball and immediately begins to press the opposing player who took possession. At the same time, Silva (21) and Fernandinho (25) begin to press the opposition on the ball by aggressively blocking the passing lanes that may be potential outlets for the player on the ball. Agüero (10) and Kompany (4) also make sure that other passing options are closed off as well.

19 MINUTES, 50 SECONDS

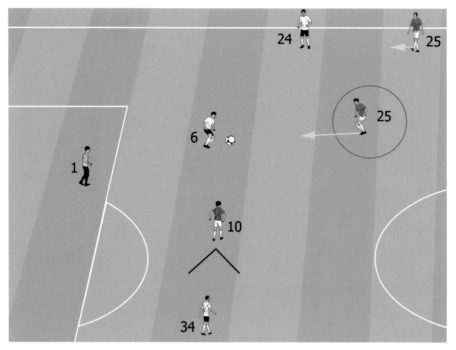

When Dynamo Kiev attempts to build out of the back, Manchester City uses Silva (21) and Agüero (10) to cut off one side of the field, allowing Manchester City to create defensive overloads by pushing their whole team over to the ball side.

This picture shows that Agüero (10) is responsible for blocking the passing lane between the two center backs, and Silva places pressure on the center back in possession. If the center back attempts to play the ball to his outside back, right winger Fernandinho is there to pressure him right away.

20 MINUTES, 1 SECOND

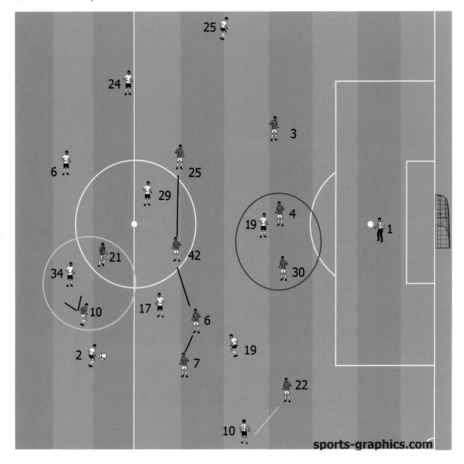

Here Manchester City is defending deep, set up in a 1-4-4-2 shape. Again, Agüero and Silva are responsible for blocking the switch while Manchester City's midfield tries to plug the middle of the field. Look how tight the midfield four are horizontally, limiting the space between the four of them centrally, but leaving the wings open. Manchester City's back four are connected to the midfield four, thus staying quite high even without pressure on the opposing ball carrier. The midfield four are tight, leaving no gaps through the central area and the back four have the two center backs, Kompany (4) and Otamendi (30), who stay central to take care of Kiev's center forward. The job of Manchester City's outside backs are to handle Kiev's wingers; the back four of Manchester City spread out horizontally, leaving gaps between the center backs and the outside backs.

25 MINUTES, 34 SECONDS

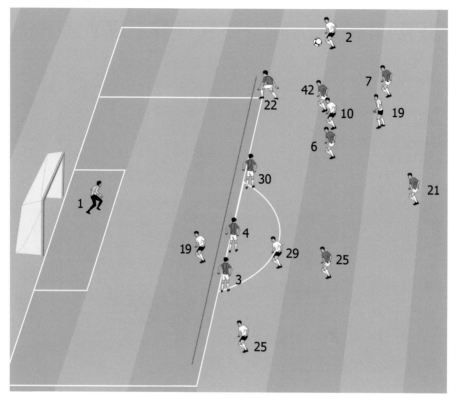

Another tactic of Manchester City is to stay out of their box for as long as possible while maintaining a defense high line. This condenses the space of Manchester City's defensive and midfield lines, making it more difficult for other teams to combine through those zones. This also makes it harder for the opposing forwards to time their runs so as to not be offside.

This picture demonstrates how the Manchester City back four are holding the 18-yard line; Kiev's players are hard pressed to find space between the Manchester City defensive and midfield lines. Furthermore, this line places the Kiev players in an offside position.

CASE STUDY #2: BEATING MANCHESTER CITY

November 21, 2015

Player Lineups for Manchester City (red) vs. Liverpool (white)

Manchester City vs. Liverpool

1:4

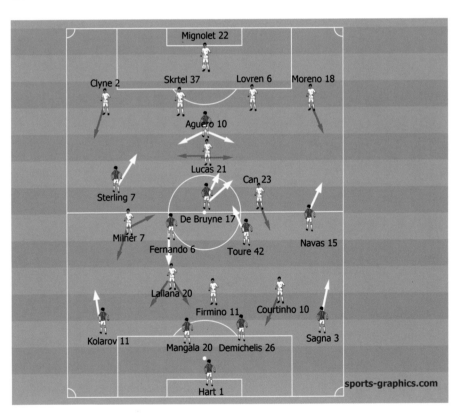

17 MINUTES, 59 SECONDS

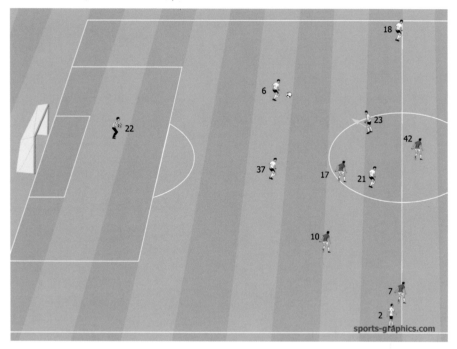

When Manchester City defends deep in a 4-4-2, Liverpool spreads their back four out while pushing the outside backs higher up the field, leaving Liverpool with two holding midfielders in front to win the ball. If Manchester City press the two center backs, Lucas (21) drops back to create a back three in the buildup play for Liverpool. Liverpool also has one offensive midfielder who looks for space between the defensive and offensive midfield lines while Liverpool's three forwards position themselves centrally to create space on the wing for Liverpool's outside backs to take advantage of.

Liverpool spreads out their back four to swing the ball in the back, creating space for Liverpool's center back, Lovren (6), to dribble up the field with the ball. Liverpool's Emre Can (23) comes to support, and Moreno (18) is high up the pitch, providing width.

18 MINUTES, 16 SECONDS

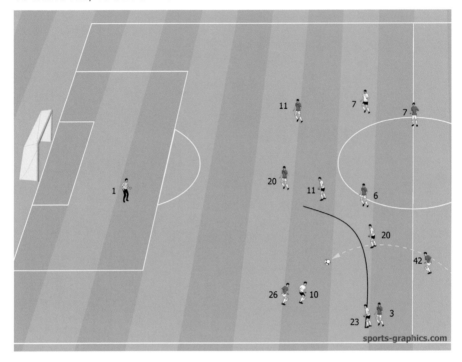

Liverpool's offensive strategy is to also use the long pass with a plan to have their midfielders and forwards set up to win the second ball. If Manchester City wins the ball, then Liverpool immediately presses them to try and win the ball back high up the field and then go straight at goal.

This picture shows the perfect setup of Liverpool; they covered every space that Manchester City could possibly head the ball. Usually, Liverpool is set up in this manner before the long ball is played in order to have the advantage of being in the right position when the second ball situation arises. Liverpool, as mentioned before, does not just simply play a long ball when under pressure from Manchester City players. Instead, they use a clever tactic of temporarily losing the ball to strategically win it back in Manchester City's half.

6 MINUTES, 50 SECONDS

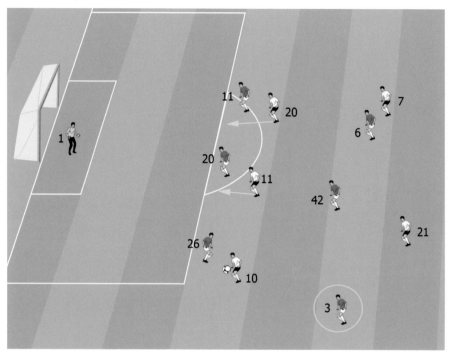

When Manchester City has possession of the ball, they push their outside backs high up the field. In response, Liverpool has their three forwards playing close together. As soon as Liverpool wins the ball, they immediately attempt to play the ball in behind Manchester City's outside backs. With the other two forwards close by, this creates a 3-v-3 or even a 3-v-2 for Liverpool.

This picture demonstrates Coutinho (10) getting behind Manchester City's outside back, Sagna (3 yellow), while the other two Liverpool forwards, Firmino and Lallana, are ready to run into the created spaces, creating a 3-v-3 on top of Manchester City's penalty box.

18 MINUTES, 27 SECONDS

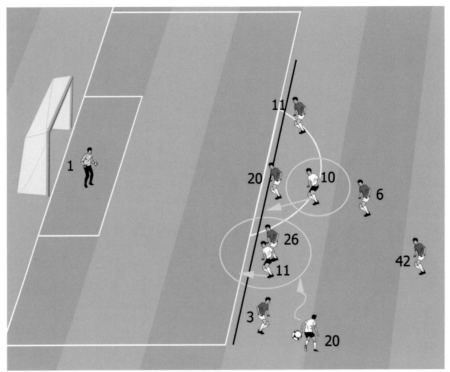

Liverpool is also focusing on Manchester City's tendency to hold a high line and to not go into their box if possible. Liverpool looks to make runs between the defenders, partly due to the individual skill and timing of their players as well as the ability to play a well-timed pass. This is likely a main reason that Liverpool uses three forwards so tight together for this game; there are more players to make those short diagonal runs in the box. This would be impossible if the forwards play on the wings, as there is just too much ground to cover.

This picture demonstrates how Manchester City attempts to hold their defensive line on top of their own box. Liverpool's Lallana (20) dribbles almost right along the top of the box, while fellow forwards, Coutinho and Firmino, (yellow) attempt to make short diagonal runs.

1 MINUTE, 12 SECONDS

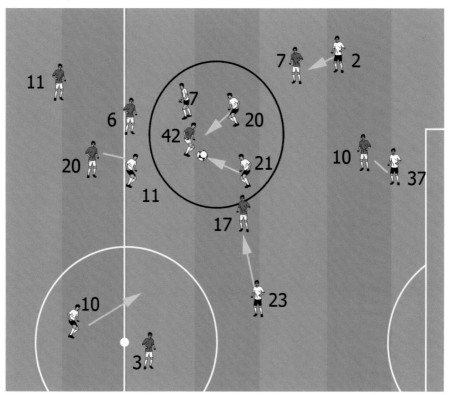

One of the main strategies implemented by Liverpool since Jürgen Klopp's arrival is using the counter-press immediately after losing the ball. The reason for this counter-press is that when a team wins the ball, they are still in a defensive shape and not yet spread out into their offensive shape. This places Liverpool in an ideal situation to win the ball back. This is particularly effective for Liverpool as they use shorter passes to attack; therefore they have multiple players around the ball if they lose it. It also means that there are multiple players around the ball to press immediately.

This picture shows Manchester City's Yaya Touré (42) win the ball from Liverpool's Milner (7) but is immediately pressed by multiple Liverpool players (in the box). Meanwhile, the other Liverpool players are covering potential outlets for Manchester City.

25 MINUTES

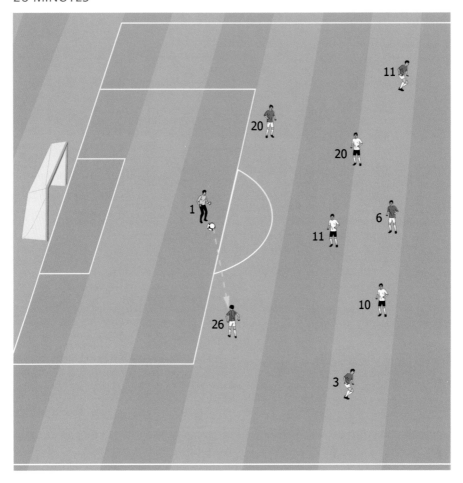

Liverpool is defending in a narrow 4-3-3 shape so they have six players centrally positioned to force Manchester City to one side of the field. Liverpool then pushes their team toward the ball and begins to press Manchester City aggressively. Liverpool are forcing Manchester City to play out of the back. After Manchester City plays the ball short to their center back, Liverpool bides their time for appropriate moments to strike, like a poor pass, a ball in the air, or playing the ball to the sides of the field. Liverpool then press Manchester City aggressively.

20 MINUTES, 33 SECONDS

When Manchester City is finally able to push Liverpool back, Liverpool's shape becomes a 1-4-5-1 as they defend deep. Liverpool's two outside forwards, Coutinho (10) and Lallana (20), join the other three Liverpool midfielders. The responsibility of Firmino (11) as the high forward is to keep Manchester City to one side, allowing the rest of the Liverpool team to push over to this side as well, thus effectively creating defensive overloads.

REAL MADRID CF

HISTORY

Real Madrid is not only the most decorated team in Spain, but also in Europe, holding the highest number of domestic titles and European successes. Founded in 1902, Real Madrid is based in Madrid at the Santiago Bernabeu, which is home to 81,000 fans. The club holds countless records, including the highest transfer fee ever for a player (Gareth Bale cost approximately 118 million Euro).[34] Worth over $3 billion, Real Madrid is perhaps the most valuable sports organization in the world, and has never been relegated from the top division in Spain (La Liga). Real Madrid has experienced various runs of success, but their most successful period was 1953-1980. During that time, Real Madrid won La Liga 18 times, the Copa del Rey five times, and the European/UEFA Champions League title six times, five of those consecutively in 1955 to 1960.

Team Motto: *Hail Madrid (unofficial).*

HONORS

★ La Liga: 32
★ Copa del Rey: 19
★ Spanish Super Cup: 9
★ European Cup/
  Champions League: 10

★ UEFA Cup: 2
★ UEFA Super Cup: 2

---

34   See en.wikipedia.org/wiki/List_of_most_expensive_association_football_transfers

REAL MADRID COACHES (2009-PRESENT)

JOSÉ MOURINHO (2009-2013)

José Mourinho was at the helm at Real Madrid from 2009 until 2013. The charismatic Portuguese manager had experienced an almost unparalleled run of success before taking over at the Bernabeu. Although Mourinho's professional playing career was very modest and short, his thirst for knowledge of the game took over shortly after his career ended and he rose quickly through the coaching ranks. His first major opportunity arose when he worked as an interpreter for English manager, Bobby Robson, at Sporting Lisbon.[35] Due to their good relationship, Mourinho followed Robson when he was hired at Barcelona.

Eventually, Mourinho's desire to be a head coach led him back to his native Portugal where he had brief spells at Benfica and Uniao de Leiria before his big break at Porto FC. It was during his time at Porto that the whole world began noticing his managerial talents. Mourinho spent only two seasons at Porto, but during that time, he took the 2003 UEFA Cup over Celtic, followed by Champions League glory after beating Monaco in the 2004 final. It was a meteoric rise to the elite of European managers. Soon, the English Premier League's Chelsea chairman, Roman Abramovich, set his sights on Mourinho to take his newly created empire to the next level.

Mourinho has since had two undeniably successful spells at Stamford Bridge though, unfortunately for Abramovich, he was never able to bring Champions League glory to West London. Mourinho did bring Chelsea home the Premier League title on three occasions as well as many other domestic trophies.

Following Mourinho's first departure from Chelsea, it only took two years to return to the top of the European hierarchy, winning the Champions League with Italy's Internazionale in 2010, defeating his old mentor, Louis van Gaal and Bayern Munich in the final. Once again, the self-anointed "Special One" was hot property in Europe, and he made the prestigious move of accepting the offer of Real Madrid's president, Florentino Perez.

---

35   *See Wikipedia.*

Real Madrid's tactical approach under Mourinho was predominantly a 4-2-3-1 formation. Regarding player personnel, he typically stuck with a rigid starting eleven. Mourinho settled on his starting eleven early in the campaign and continued with that group, injuries permitting.

Mourinho is notorious for winning, and it seems that he does not particularly care how he achieves this success. Before Mourinho's arrival, Madrid typically played a possession-oriented offensive style. It took just weeks for Mourinho to transition them into a team known for their high aggression, tremendous counter-attacks, and the capability to adjust tactically, depending on the opponent.

Mourhino was known to make adjustments that depended on the weakness of the opposition; this was most evident by his tinkering of the midfield setup. For example, it was impossible to predict how high he let his team press, and whether or not he would man mark certain players on the opposition. Looking at the midfield setup, Mourinho preferred to play with two holding midfielders or even three defensively oriented midfielders, especially during big games.

Mourinho's pressing style during his stay at Madrid was dependent on who his opposition was on game day; it included counter-pressing, high pressing on the opponent's back four, or sitting back in midfield and allowing the other team to possess the ball in their own half. As a result, it was impossible to predict the approach Mourinho would use, but there was usually a well thought out reason for a particular setup. Mourinho would also go so far as to instruct his team to play the ball long to ensure they did not lose the ball in their own half, a prospect that made many of the Real Madrid fans very unhappy, especially during the "El Classico" against FC Barcelona when the counter-press from Barcelona was trying to be avoided this way.

Mourinho was released from Real Madrid in 2013 to move back to Chelsea. He was let go from Chelsea in 2015, and is now with Manchester United.

HONORS AT REAL MADRID
★ La Liga: 1
★ Copa del Rey: 1
★ Supercopa de Espana: 1

CARLO ANCELOTTI (2013-2015)

The 56-year-old Italian was a great player in his own right before starting his managerial career. He made over 300 league appearances in his native Italy, predominantly playing for Roma and AC Milan where he won the European Cup on two occasions. Carlo Ancelotti even earned 26 caps for his country and was a member of the squad that finished third at the 1990 World Cup.

Ancelotti's managerial career began with Reggiana in Italy's Serie "B" in 1995. His reputation grew when he took charge of Parma and led them to a second place finish in the Serie "A" and qualified for the Champions League. He then moved on to Juventus where, despite a solid overall record, the lack of silverware ultimately frustrated the management and Ancelotti was released in 2001.

At this juncture Ancelotti returned to his former club, AC Milan, and embarked on the most successful period of his managerial career to date. While at the San Siro, he won the Champions League in 2003 through a tantalizing penalty shootout win over his former club, Juventus. He also won the Champions League in 2007 when his side edged out Liverpool.

Ancelotti then moved on to England and was welcomed by Chelsea. It was here that he won the Premier League title following his first year at the helm. However, a disappointing second season left him soured in the eyes of Abramovich and he was let go in 2011. The Italian then joined French giants, Paris Saint Germain, and won the Ligue 1 in his first full season before requesting permission to join Real Madrid following the departure of Mourinho.

Ancelotti's tactical approach with Real Madrid did not change quite as much as it did under Mourinho. Ancelotti typically kept to a similar setup and made only small adjustments, if any, on a game-to-game basis. He was a firm believer in possessing the ball as much as possible, and aimed to control and win the game in this manner.

After taking the helm at Real Madrid, Ancelotti changed the counter-attacking style, and moved the system into a 4-2-2-2 shape, using two clear forwards in Ronaldo and Benzema. The outside backs played much higher than they did under Mourinho. The defensive organization that Ancelotti brought to Real Madrid may be partly accounted to his Italian roots, as Italian coaches are known for their great defensive organization, and Ancelotti was certainly no different in that regard.

Ancelotti tended to favor a less aggressive, but highly organized pressing style. When certain triggers were activated, such as when the ball was played to the side, the team transitioned to that side to win the ball back. This approach was fairly consistent throughout his time at Madrid, although he switched his 4-2-2-2/4-4-2 system towards the end of his reign to a 4-3-3 to highlight the strengths of Bale, Ronaldo, and Benzema, the main threats going forward.

Ancelotti will take over for Pep Guardiola at Bayern Munich at the beginning of the 2016-2017 season.

HONORS AT REAL MADRID
★ UEFA Champions League: 1
★ UEFA Super Cup: 1
★ FIFA Club World Cup: 1
★ Copa del Rey: 1

RAFA BENITEZ (2015-2016)

Although the Spaniard spent only a brief period at the Bernabeu, Rafa Benitez's managerial pedigree still remains one of the strongest around. Benitez was an unspectacular player so he quickly began to focus on the coaching side of the game from a young age. At just 26 years of age, Benitez took over the Real Madrid "B" squad, winning the league title twice.

His first steps into senior management away from Madrid were not easy for Benitez, but once he was hired by Tenerife and immediately earned them a promotion to the Spanish La Liga, his reputation was firmly established.

Benitez then moved to Valencia CF where his career truly took off. His influence at La Mestalla was impressive to say the least. In 2002, he won the club's first La Liga title in 31 years at the conclusion of his first season. Despite a mediocre second season, Benitez's team bounced back to win another La Liga title in 2004 as well as the UEFA Cup. However, Benitez had a falling out with the ownership, resulting in his resignation. Benitez was immediately hired by Liverpool Football Club to replace Gerard Houllier. Benitez stayed at Liverpool from 2004-2010.

Once again, Benitez wasted no time in massively impacting Liverpool. He managed to convince the inspirational club captain, Steven Gerrard, to stay, and he signed former player, Luis Garcia as well as the immensely talented midfielder Xabi Alonso to bolster his squad. Despite a league campaign that was undeniably disappointing, Benitez did the unthinkable and made these sleeping giants a force to be reckoned with once again on the European stage. The 2005 Champions League final win over AC Milan will go down as one of the greatest games of all time, as Benitez orchestrated an unlikely comeback from 0-3 down at halftime to beat the Italians on penalties. It was the club's fifth European Cup in total, but the first since 1984.

Benitez then moved on to Inter Milan for a short (and trying) spell, lasting just one season despite winning the FIFA World Club Championship. He then masterminded a Europa League win in 2013 for Chelsea, but once again his stay there was short. Benitez's last stop prior to Real Madrid was in Italy with Napoli. He stayed at Napoli for two seasons, winning the Coppa Italia in his first campaign.

After Napoli, Benitez went to Real Madrid, but only lasted four months; he was let go in January 2016.

HONORS AT REAL MADRID
★   None

ZINEDINE ZIDANE (2016-PRESENT)

As a player, Zinedine Zidane, was widely considered to be one of the most talented players to grace the playing surface. A stylish midfield player, there was very little that Zidane could not do with the ball at his feet. He was graceful and technical, and played the game at his very leisurely pace, yet rarely could anyone get near him.

His career can be split fairly evenly between stops at three different teams: Girondins de Bordeaux in his native France, Juventus in Italy, and finally at Real Madrid. Zidane won almost every title that a club player can win. He won Serie "A" on two occasions, La Liga once, and the Champions League in 2002, scoring one of the greatest goals of all time and leading Los Blancos to victory over Bayer Leverkusen in the final.

Zidane has made over 100 appearances for the French National team, scoring 31 goals. He was also a member of the French squad that won the 1998 World Cup and the European Championships in 2000. His two goals in the 1998 final inspired his team to victory over the highly favored Brazilian opponents. Zidane nearly won a second World Cup in 2006, having dragged his team to the final. He scored an early penalty in the decider before his team fell to Italy on penalty kicks. One of the hallmarks of that final game is Zidane's infamous clash with Italian defender, Marco Materazzi.

Zidane's managerial career began as an assistant to Carlo Ancelotti in 2013. He then took over the Real Madrid "B" team in 2014 to complete his coaching credentials before being hired as the head coach in 2016, following Benitez.

HONORS AT REAL MADRID AS AN ASSISTANT
★   Copa del Rey: 1
★   UEFA Champions League: 1

REAL MADRID'S KEY PLAYERS

PEPE (2007-PRESENT)

The 33-year-old Pepe began his youth career in his native Brazil, but decided to move to Maritimo, a club in Portugal, to start his professional career. His performance at Maritimo earned him a transfer to FC Porto in 2004 where he began to establish himself as an up-and-coming center back in Europe. It was during his spell at FC Porto that Real Madrid came in search of his services. Since his debut for Real Madrid in 2007, Pepe has been ever-present in their squad and has made over 200 league appearances[36] in the process.

---

36 *Ibid.*

The 6'2" Pepe is primarily known for his physical brand of defending. He is an unscrupulous defender, often looking to push the boundaries of legal defending. As a result, Pepe often receives disciplinary action, which has been a constant problem throughout his career.

During Mourinho's stay at Real Madrid, Pepe mainly played as a center back, but was deployed to a central midfield role on several occasions to break up play of opponents. This move was due to his incredible work ethic and physical presence.

One of his standout performances as a holding midfielder was during the 2011 Copa del Rey final in which Real Madrid won against Barcelona. Barcelona's midfielder, Xavi, was responsible for Barcelona's buildup in the midfield third, and was considered one of the masters of his craft at the time. Mourinho assigned Pepe the task of man-marking Xavi during this game. This disrupted Barcelona's buildup play immensely. The Pepe–Mourinho duo was a match made in heaven because they both brought massive amounts of passion to the game.

When Carlo Ancelotti arrived, Real Madrid's physical game changed and they were known more for possessing in the back. While Pepe is still above average in terms of possession skills, he did not flourish as much because his true strengths were no longer as emphasized.

SERGIO RAMOS (2005-PRESENT)

Despite being a loyal Real Madrid servant since 2005, Sergio Ramos actually rose through the ranks at Sevilla, first as a youth player and then as a first team regular. His impressive performances caught the eye of Real Madrid and he moved to the Bernabeu for one of the biggest fees ever paid for a teenager.

The 6'0" Ramos began his career as a right back but has moved into the center of the defense in recent years, even making the occasional appearance in a central midfield role. Ramos is the prototypical modern day defender. He may not be the biggest in stature, but he is an insanely talented athlete. Ramos possesses above-average technical ability, but perhaps his best quality is the combination of his leadership, passion, and sheer will to win. He has been the captain for Real Madrid since the departure of legendary goalkeeper, Iker Casillas. Ramos often frustrates opponents with his antics, but he is also the type of player everyone would like on their team. Similar to Pepe, Ramos shares some disciplinary issues, which have often been a weakness throughout his career.

Ramos has been a fairly consistent goal threat from set pieces throughout his career. Perhaps his most infamous goal was his late equalizer against local rivals Atletico in the 2014 Champions League final, which Real Madrid won in extra time. Ramos has now won the majority of available trophies in club soccer.

Looking at his role under the recent coaches at Real Madrid, Ramos's position as a center back tends to remain constant. He was a primary starter under Mourinho's more direct physical style of play as well as under the coaches who have followed. His versatile skill set makes him a highly valued asset to the team due to his ability to adapt seamlessly, regardless of the coach in charge at the time and the tactical style they adopt.

MARCELO (2007-PRESENT)

This 27-year-old Brazilian left back has been at Real Madrid since 2007. Marcelo has been a consistent presence in the starting eleven of Real Madrid since his transfer from Brazil's club, Fluminense, amassing over 250 league appearances for Real Madrid. Marcelo has appeared over 40 times for his country. During this time, he has won the Confederations Cup in 2013 and was part of the 2014 squad that reached the semifinal of the World Cup.

Marcelo is predominantly known as an offensively gifted fullback. His dribbling skills are very good and he has an above average ability to cross and link up with his teammates in the final third. Since Cristiano Ronaldo came to Real Madrid, the left side of Real Madrid's squad has been known for their strong combination play.

Marcelo and Ronaldo's skills seem to perfectly complement each other. When Marcelo is pushing high and going on one of his famous dribbling attacks into the opposing final third, Ronaldo will look to open up spaces for Marcelo to run into.

Ronaldo and Marcelo are both excellent in combining with each other because of their brilliant technical skills. Marcelo has been an integral member of the Real Madrid side under all of the coaches since his arrival. Perhaps the only aspect of Marcelo's game that was adjusted was how high he would play when Real Madrid was in possession, but this was on a game-to-game basis.

Marcelo was perhaps the greatest threat under Ancelotti's 4-2-2-2 system, in which the outside backs went as high as the opposing back four to provide width for the attack.

LUKA MODRIC (2012-PRESENT)

The diminutive Luka Modric has established a reputation over his long career as one of the most creative midfield players in world soccer. This 30-year-old began his career in his native Croatia but was soon snapped up by Tottenham Hotspur in 2008 following a string of impressive performances for Dinamo Zagreb and the Croatian national team. He was named in the Team of the Tournament in the 2008 UEFA European Championship with Croatia but had a slow start in his career in London. However, it wasn't long before Modric was again demonstrating his brilliant creative ability. After four impressive years with Tottenham Hotspur, he was signed by Real Madrid in a big money deal. Modric has played 87 times for Croatia at three major tournaments, scoring ten goals in the process. He is the only Croatian-born player to be named to the FIFA World XI squad and is the second Croatian to be named to the Team of the Tournament squad in the Euros. He has won the Best Croatian Player Award on four occasions and also won the 2003 Bosnian League Player of the Year.[37]

Modric is mainly known as a playmaker in midfield, facilitating goal-scoring opportunities for his teammates. However, he is also capable of scoring many different types of goals. He is a wonderfully quick operator, using his low center of gravity to effortlessly move around the field. Modric continues to improve with age, having recently been named in the 2015 FIFA Pro XI for the first time in his career.

Modric's skill set is best suited to a coach and team who prefer a passing and possession oriented game. Modric benefited immensely from the way in which Carlo

---

37   *Ibid.*

Ancelotti set up the team. After the first few weeks under Zidane, who provides a high degree of freedom to his players, it is evident that his philosophy is to control the game through passing, attempting to dominate for the majority of the match. It is likely that Modric will also flourish under Zidane's tutelage.

GARETH BALE (2013-PRESENT)

The Welshman Gareth Bale was earmarked as a top talent early in his life. He came through the academy system at Southampton, making his debut at just 16 years old. He played only one full Championship season at St Mary's as a left back before the Premier League's Tottenham Hotspur signed him. Bale had a slow start to life at White Hart Lane as he struggled to adjust to his new surroundings. Bale has also enjoyed a solid international career with Wales. He has already played 54 times for his country, scoring 19 goals in the process. Most impressively, Bale almost single-handedly led the Dragons to qualify for Euro 2016, scoring many big goals in the qualifying campaign.

It wasn't until the 2010-2011 season, when Bale was moved to left wing, that his career took off and he became one of the most feared wingers in the game. His combination of blistering pace, good size, and a brilliant left foot made him extremely difficult to defend against. His performance against Inter Milan during the 2010 Champions League group phase made him a household name throughout Europe.

During Bale's final season at White Hart Lane, he was voted Professional Footballers' Association's (PFA) Player of the Year after an outstanding campaign, scoring over 20 goals. He was arguably considered the most dangerous player in the league. It was after this season that he made his transfer to Real Madrid following a world record transfer fee.

During his first couple of seasons with Real Madrid, Bale has been used mainly as a right winger. His role was to drift inside to the half space when Madrid's right outside back would go high, providing the width on the right side. When Bale would receive the ball in that space, he ideally looked to create 1-v-1 or even 1-v-2 situations, cutting inside to shoot with his incredibly lethal left foot. Since the appointment of Zinedine Zidane, there has been frequent interchanging of the three forwards: Ronaldo, Benzema, and Bale.

KARIM BENZEMA (2009-PRESENT)

The 28-year-old Karim Benzema has been ever-present for Real Madrid since joining from Olympique Lyon in 2009. During his time in France, Benzema established himself as one of Europe's top young strikers. This form has continued seamlessly since his move to the Bernabeu. Benzema has represented France over 80 times, scoring 27 goals for his country since his debut in 2007.

Frenchman Benzema is a classic number nine. At 6'2" and powerfully built, Benzema is a handful for any defender he faces. Along with being technically solid, his finishing ability separates him from most. He has scored at least 20 goals in eight of the last nine seasons. Perhaps even more impressive about this number of goals is that one of his main roles as the forward for Real Madrid is to create space for Ronaldo, facilitating his goal scoring opportunities.

Benzema is a major threat when playing on the counter-attack due to his speed and direct approach. One of the primary reasons that Benzema did well under Mourinho was that in the bigger games, Mourinho preferred to sit back and let the opponent come at them.

When Mourinho favored the slower offensive buildup approach, Benzema was not always first choice, instead falling behind Gonzalo Higuain in the pecking order. Since Mourinho's departure, Benzema once again became the first choice in all situations under every coach that followed.

Benzema is quite adept at reading situations quickly, skillfully knowing when to make a run, shoot, or lay a ball off. He possesses the type of consistency and longevity that is rare but extremely valuable.

CRISTIANO RONALDO (2009-PRESENT)

The 31-year-old Cristiano Ronaldo has unquestionably been one of the top two players in the world for the better part of the past decade. This Portuguese international had a brief spell early in his career with Sporting Lisbon, having graduated from their academy before Sir Alex Ferguson spotted his outrageous talent and brought him to Manchester United in 2003.

Ronaldo was signed by Real Madrid in 2009 and the improvements kept on coming for him. As good as Ronaldo was at Old Trafford, he was even better at the Bernabeu, averaging more than a goal per game during his now 200+ league appearances for the club. Standing at 6'1", Ronaldo is strong, lightning fast, agile, and technically gifted. He can shoot equally well with both feet and is a threat in the air due to his unbelievable vertical leap and offensive timing in the box.

Ronaldo and Mourinho seemed to be a perfect match when they were brought together at the Beranbeu. Mourinho prefers a more vertical game and Ronaldo's strengths seemed to be made for that type of system. Mourhino was the first coach to reduce Ronaldo's defensive responsibilities, the primary reason being that he didn't want Ronaldo to become fatigued. This strategy also had the added of benefit of keeping Ronaldo higher up the field; when Madrid did regain possession, Ronaldo would have more space to exploit.

Ronaldo played mostly on the left wing under Mourinho, which allowed him to dribble inside and look to finish on his dominant right foot. Ronaldo is well-known for shooting on sight if there is even the slightest chance to unleash.

As previously mentioned when talking about Marcelo, the left side at Real Madrid is well-known for the Ronaldo–Marcelo tandem team because they complement each other so well. This was particularly evident when the coaches who succeeded Mourinho also used Ronaldo in a similar manner, starting him on the left wing or as a deeper hanging forward on the left side. They would also give Ronaldo more freedom when defending so as to be ready to attack immediately and effectively when Real Madrid won the ball.

Ronaldo has won almost every individual and team accolade available at club level. His credentials and awards are almost incomparable in the modern generation and can only be matched by FC Barcelona winger, Lionel Messi.

GENERAL SETUP UNDER ZINEDINE ZIDANE

OFFENSIVE

Given Zidane's new leadership at the Bernabeu, it is difficult at this stage to determine what he is trying to achieve with this Real Madrid team. However, it is clearly evident that he places high priority on attacking through possession. When Real Madrid has clear possession of the ball, they are set up in a 4-3-3 system and attempt to build up from the back.

When Madrid builds up from the back, the two center backs spread to the edge of the box while the outside backs push higher up the field. These outside backs do not push as high as the forwards, but instead position themselves as high as the Real Madrid holding midfielder or even the offensive midfielder. The outside backs position themselves all the way to the touchline to provide as much width as possible for the rest of the team.

In the midfield, Zidane has given the players the freedom to interchange, forcing the opposition to alter their position as a result of their own smart movements. His midfield is generally set up with a holding midfielder and two offensive midfielders when in possession of the ball. The holding midfielder—typically Toni Kroos—will at times drop back between the two center backs. The two offensive midfielders have different tendencies, depending on who is playing in a particular game. Zidane has so far preferred to play with Isco as the left offensive midfielder and Modric as the right offensive midfielder. As Zidane allows each player more freedom, the natural tendencies of the players become clearer. While Modric prefers to open up play a lot, he will also drift toward the holding midfielder, or even further back, receiving the ball next to the right center back. On the contrary, Isco may drift more into the higher regions of the field. He may be level with the opposing back four, or even making runs in behind them to stretch the other team when possible.

The three forwards are usually set up with two members of the trio acting as wing forwards, providing width to the attack until the outside backs are in position to take on that role. Once the outside backs are available to provide the width, the two wing forwards will then drift inside, taking the opposing outside backs with them. This creates more space on the wings for the outside backs to push forward. The three forwards will interchange with each other quite frequently, even occasionally overloading the side with two or all three of them simultaneously. Zidane's preferred choice thus far has been to position Ronaldo on the left wing to use his speed to dribble inside toward his strong foot, Benzema in the middle as a natural center forward, and Bale or James on the right flank.

Although it is still very early in the Zidane era, it is already clear that he prefers to control the game through possession. He will attempt this by using short passes in the opponent's half while also giving the players the freedom to be creative.

DEFENSIVE

A major characteristic of Zidane's approach is a noticeably higher intensity in pressing once Madrid loses the ball. Once a Real Madrid player loses possession of the ball, multiple players aggressively pressure the opposing player with the ball in an attempt to win it back right away. Another option is to force the other team to play the ball long. A distinct difference between Zidane's squad and those before him is that he requires all of the players to be involved in the process of winning the ball back, even Ronaldo, Bale, or Benzema.

Real Madrid uses a 4-3-3 defensive shape when the other team builds up from the back. The Madrid center forward is responsible for pressing the center back with possession of the ball, forcing him to either go long or choose a side as the other Madrid players attempt to close down the middle of the field.

If the opponent chooses a side of the field, the Madrid wide forward and outside back usually place high pressure on the opponent's outside back and winger. The rest of the team shift over to the ball side of the field, making the field more compact and closing off any potential options for the player on the ball.

When teams do move into Madrid's defensive third, Madrid sets up in a 4-4-2 shape and one of the wide forwards—typically not Ronaldo—joins the midfield three. The primary goal at this point is to keep those two lines horizontally and vertically as compact as possible in the central area. This forces the opposing team to play the ball wide, which allows Madrid to shift over to the side of the opposing ball carrier.

As mentioned earlier in the offensive setup, it is still early in the Zidane era to fully analyze his approach, but again, his preference to control the game, even when defending, is evident. The high emphasis on pressing the opponent immediately has been obvious since his first game.

CASE STUDY #1:
A REAL MADRID WIN

January 31, 2016

Player Lineups for Real Madrid (white) vs. Espanyol Barcelona (red) (with player tendencies)

Real Madrid vs. Espanyol Barcelona

6:0

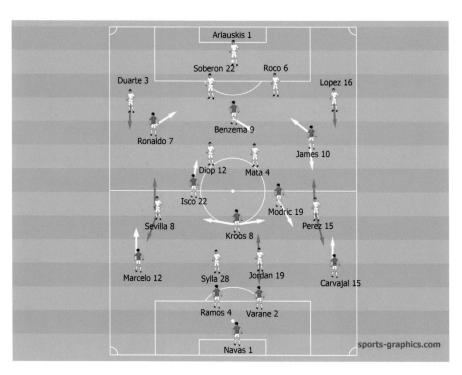

26 SECONDS

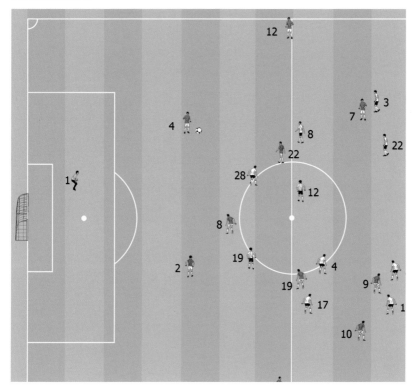

Real Madrid set up in a 1-4-3-3 system when they are looking to build up from the back. In this particular system, the center backs spread wide to receive the ball while the Madrid outside backs push as high as the offensive midfielders, also providing width.

The midfield three are typically set up with a holding midfielder, who forms a triangle with the two center backs and the two offensive center midfielders.

The two wing forwards also provide width, at least until the outside backs are in position. When this occurs, the wing forwards drift inside, taking the opposing outside backs inside with them. This creates space on the flank for the Madrid outside backs.

As this picture demonstrates, Madrid center backs Ramos (4) and Varane (2) start the buildup with Toni Kroos (8), who is in the holding midfield position. Modric (19) and Isco (22) are positioned in the half spaces, and the forward line of Ronaldo (7), Benzema (9), and James (10) drifts to the middle to occupy the opposing back four. This creates space on the wing.

141

41 SECONDS

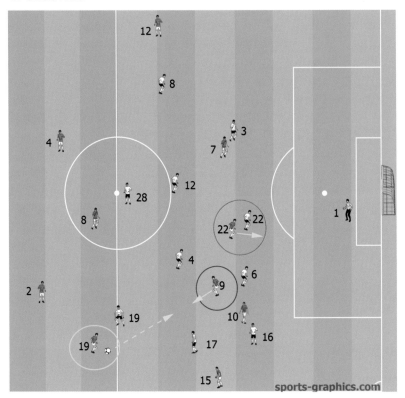

Zidane provides a lot of freedom for the Real Madrid players to interchange positions during the build-up phase. This freedom can create confusion for the opponent while opening space for other Madrid players to use.

This picture shows Modric (19) checking back into the space that Carvajal (15)—the Madrid right back—created by pushing up field and taking the Espanyol players out of position. The interchanging is also taking place; Madrid's center forward Benzema (9) checks to the ball while Isco (22)—the Madrid offensive center midfielder—transitions from the midfield to the center forward position.

The Espanyol players must now make a decision: either place pressure on Modric (19) due to the interchanging of positions or follow the runs of Isco (22), or Benzema (9). Espanyol stayed in their two banks of four instead of going with the Madrid players, making it possible for Benzema (9) to receive the ball between the defensive and midfield lines.

4 MINUTES, 45 SECONDS

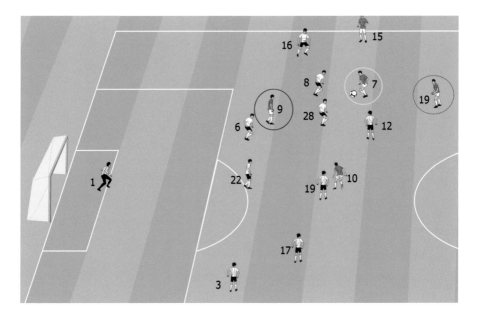

With Zidane's approach, the top three can freely move and may aim to overload particular sections of the field. This assists them in combining effectively to the opposing goal.

In this example, Ronaldo (7) switches sides with James (10) and drifts into the half space with the ball. At the same time, James (10) drops into the center midfield position, while Benzema (9) drifts over and checks to the center forward position.

Modric (19) provides support in the back while Madrid's right back, Carvajal (15), creates width on the right side. This creates several open passing lanes for Madrid and a perfect overload situation for Zidane's side.

5 MINUTES

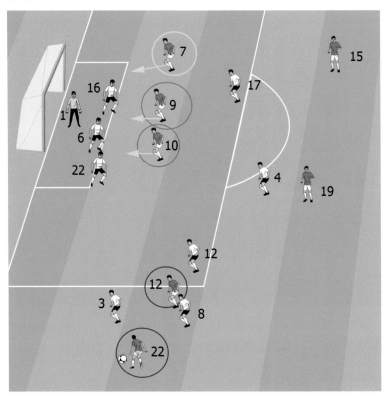

When Madrid does break through on the flank, they typically have all three of their forwards in front of the goal. Ronaldo, Bale, James, and Benzema are natural goal scorers. In other words, they will make every attempt to get into the box and finish off the attack. With these players in the box when the ball is on the flank, the opposing team must make a decision whether to persist with keeping their back four horizontally compact to push to the ball on the flank, which may open up space at the back post. The other alternative would be to man mark, possibly leaving gaps horizontally.

This picture shows that Isco (22) and Marcelo (12) broke through on the left flank and were prepared to cross into the Espanyol box. All three forwards from Madrid,— Ronaldo (7), James (10), and Benzema (9)—are positioned in front of the goal, giving themselves the best opportunity to finish the attack off with a goal. Espanyol's back four attempt to stay connected horizontally, but this leaves Ronaldo open at the back post, a dangerous position.

19 MINUTES, 31 SECONDS

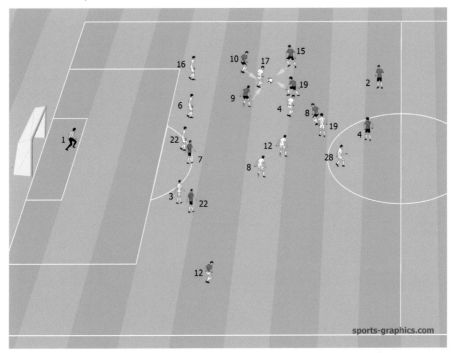

Zidane's strategy for the transition from offense to defense is to press the ball carrier immediately, using multiple players. When Madrid lost the ball, four of their players placed high pressure on the Espanyol ball carrier. This forced him to go long, helping Madrid regain possession of the ball and start their next attack.

19 MINUTES, 46 SECONDS

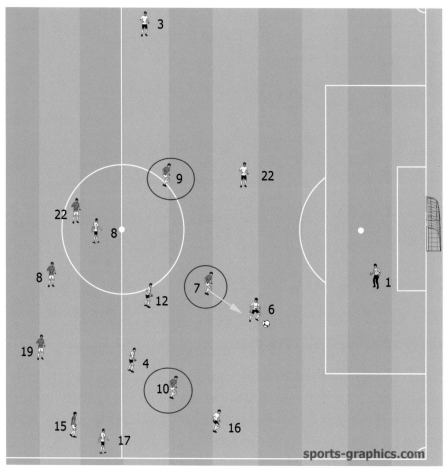

When Espanyol was in their build-up phase, Madrid set up in a 4-3-3 shape. They used the central forward to pressure the center back with the ball, forcing the Espanyol center back to one side.

After Espanyol chose the left side, the Madrid outside back immediately pressures the left wing forward, while Madrid's right forward pressures the left outside back. The rest of the Madrid team transitions over to ball side.

This picture demonstrates that Madrid is set up in a 4-3-3 shape. Ronaldo (7) is the center forward who pressures the opposing center back. Carvajal (15)—Madrid's right back—takes care of the Espanyol's left winger and James (10) is ready to pressure the Espanyol right back.

3 MINUTES, 46 SECONDS

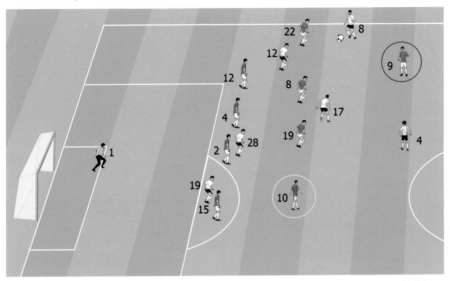

When Madrid needs to defend from deep, they set up in a 4-4-2 shape with the aim of keeping the middle of the field compact. Once Espanyol decides which side they'll play toward, both lines of the defensive four aggressively shift over to the ball side.

This picture demonstrates that Espanyol tries to play down the right side of the field and Madrid's back four have shifted over to ball side accordingly. Madrid's midfield four consists of the three midfield players pushing over to the ball side while James (10), the right forward, drops back to join the midfield three, creating a more horizontally compact midfield four. The two Madrid forwards are simultaneously trying to make life difficult for the Espanyol players who are attempting to pass the ball back to an outlet. The two Madrid forwards are also preparing for the counter-attack in the event that Madrid wins the ball back.

CASE STUDY #2: BEATING REAL MADRID

February 27, 2016

Player Lineups for Real Madrid (red) vs. Atletico Madrid (white) (with player tendencies)

Real Madrid vs. Atletico Madrid

0:1

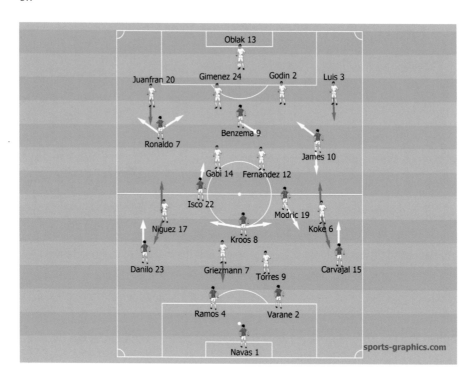

22 SECONDS

Atletico Madrid's primary defensive strategy against Real Madrid was to defend high up the field while set in a 4-4-2 shape. Under their coach Simeone, Atletico Madrid aimed to place Real Madrid under high pressure all over the field. Atletico tends to be proactive in their defending; they attempt to lead the opposing team where they want them to go and do not defend reactively. Atletico does not wait and see what the other team does offensively and then react to that strategy.

This picture shows that Real Madrid is in their build-up shape, trying to possess with their two center backs. Atletico's two forwards are each responsible for one of the Real Madrid center backs with the intention of putting serious pressure on the ball carrier. The Atletico midfield four move to the side where Real Madrid is looking to break through, condensing the space around the ball as much as possible.

1 MINUTE, 9 SECONDS

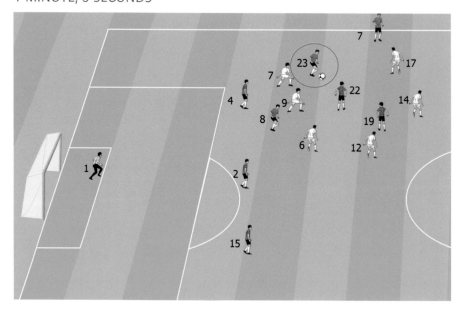

Atletico has now successfully pushed Real Madrid to one side of the field, leaving them with only limited areas to potentially play the ball to. Atletico overloads that side of the field, reducing Real Madrid's options even more.

Real Madrid possesses the ball on the left side. Atletico then pushes over six of their players to overload this area. The Atletico midfielders are responsible for condensing the space around the ball while the forwards back-press the Real Madrid player with the ball. The ultimate goal is to either force Real Madrid to play the ball long or for Atletico to win the ball high up the field, starting their own attack.

20 MINUTES, 3 SECONDS

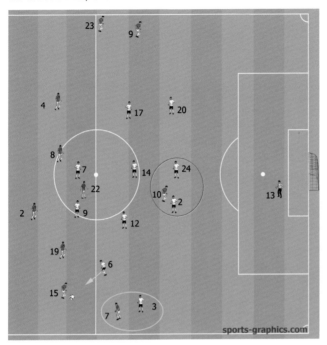

If Atletico is defending in the midfield area and their initial high pressure is broken, they will revert back to the 4-4-2 setup. The two forwards keep close together in the area where Real Madrid's holding midfielder is positioned. At the same time, Atletico tries to keep their four midfielders high and horizontally compact in order to close down the middle.

The Atletico back four are also vertically compact with the rest of their team. The aim at this point is to not allow Real Madrid to play between the defensive and midfield line. Their back four mark Real Madrid forwards rather than looking to stay horizontally compact. The Atletico outside backs mark the Real Madrid wing forwards (yellow circle) while the two center backs cover the central forward (red circle), even if it leaves gaps between the back four. This forces Real Madrid to play to one side of the field, where Atletico can push over to start their intense pressure again.

This picture shows the vertical compactness of the entire Atletico team in their 4-4-2 shape. Due to the Atletico forwards and midfielder closing down the middle of the field, Real Madrid can only play the ball to the side. Atletico's Luiz marks Ronaldo while the two center backs stay in the center to watch Benzema, rather than staying connected to Luiz. While the ball is traveling to Real Madrid's right back, the Atletico midfield four and the two forwards are now in a full sprint over to ball-side.

14 MINUTES, 46 SECONDS

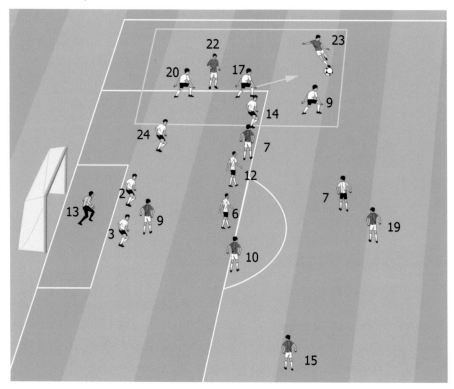

When Atletico defends deep against Real Madrid, their same defensive principles apply. They continue to maintain vertical compactness, but they also have specific man-marking assignments. This means that when they defend deep, the man marker may not stay as connected to the back four.

This picture demonstrates Atletico defending all the way back to the top of their own box. Yet they continue to stay compact vertically due to the fact that, under their coach Simeone, all eleven players are expected to defend. This can be seen as Atletico forces Real Madrid to the wing, creating a 4-v-2 overload while defending. They maintain a good defensive shape inside the box as every Real Madrid player is being marked tightly by at least one Atletico player.

5 MINUTES, 56 SECONDS

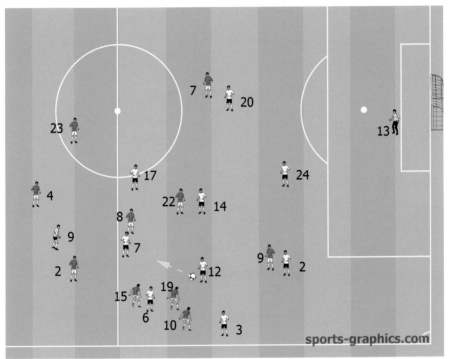

When Atletico transitions from defense to offense, they use their defensive structure as their offensive structure and vice versa. When defending, Atletico overloads the areas around the ball as much as possible. When they transition to attack, they now have multiple players around the ball.

Atletico is a high-level technically proficient team; their players have elite passing abilities even under extreme pressure. When Atletico wins the ball, they attempt to play their way out of pressure with short passes to counter immediately rather than playing out of pressure by opening up as a team.

Due to the attacking setup of Atletico, they can easily transition back to their original defensive shape and counter press immediately if Real Madrid wins the ball back.

This picture demonstrates how Atletico has overloaded Real Madrid's left side. As soon as Atletico regains possession of the ball, they attempt to play through Real Madrid by forward passes to immediately counter.

18 MINUTES, 14 SECONDS

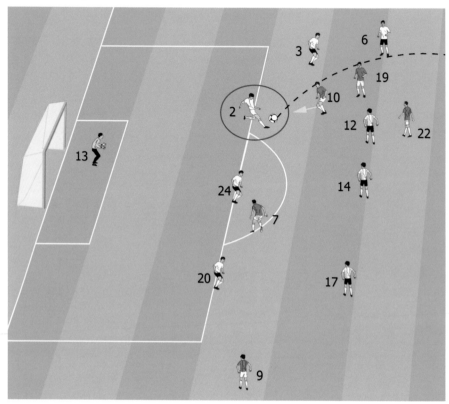

When Real Madrid pressures Atletico in their defensive third, Atletico does not take risks in that area, even if it means simply clearing the ball long up the field.

This picture shows that Atletico's left center back is immediately pressured by Real Madrid as soon as he receives the ball. This Atletico defender is not taking any chances whatsoever by playing out of the back. Instead, he decides to play the long ball up the field, clearing it immediately and reducing the pressure.

15 MINUTES, 44 SECONDS

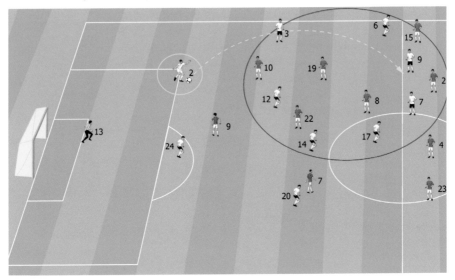

Even if Real Madrid does not pressure Atletico when they have the ball in the back, Atletico will take full advantage of that lack of pressure, setting up their whole team to one side of the field. The Atletico defender on the ball is able to play a long pass into that specific area of the field, providing his team the option to either win the first ball or, at the very worst, win the second ball since they have completely overloaded that particular area of the field.

This means that for the duration of the game against Atletico, Real Madrid is either in possession of the ball or the game is in constant transition. The reason for this is that when Atletico attacked, they either transitioned by countering right away through combination play; or when they had possession, they aimed to move their players high up the field as soon as possible, to play a long pass even if it meant losing the ball. Once they were in Real Madrid's half, they immediately looked to win the ball back.

This picture demonstrates that there is no imminent pressure or even attempted pressure from Real Madrid on Atletico's left center back. The entire Atletico team can now shift over to the ball-side, preparing to win the first or the second ball. Atletico's left center back then plays the long ball over Real Madrid's forward and midfield line.

CREDITS

Cover design: Andreas Reuel

Coverphotos: ©picture-alliance/dpa

Graphics: www.sports-graphics.com

Photos: ©picture-alliance/dpa: pg. s. 47, 21, 71, 81 105, 139

Layout &
Typesetting: Andreas Reuel

Copyediting: Anne Rumery

DISCOVER AN ENTERTAINING HISTORY OF SOCCER!

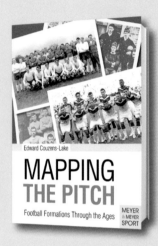

Edward Couzens-Lake

MAPPING THE PITCH

Football Formations Through The Ages

This book is an informative yet informal and entertaining exploration of the history and evolution of football formations and tactics from the earliest days of the Victorian age gentleman 'players' to the successes—and failures—of the 2014 World Cup in Brazil.

Mapping The Pitch analyses and explains the thinking behind the popular formations and tactics that came with the introduction of semi-organised play and shows how the thinking behind the game changed with the steady implementation of rule changes in football from the late 19th century onwards, specifically one which remains amongst the most contentious in the game to this day: the offside law. The book also explores how the game might have evolved, changed and existed today if the offside law had never been implemented.

304 p.,b/w,

31 photos, 13 illustrations,

paperback

5 3/4" x 8 1/4"

ISBN: 9781782550600

$ 14.95 US/$ 22.95 AUS

£ 9.95 UK/€14.95

All information subject to change. © Thinkstock/iStockphoto

MEYER & MEYER Sport
Von-Coels-Str. 390
52080 Aachen
Germany

Phone	+49 02 41 - 9 58 10 - 13
Fax	+49 02 41 - 9 58 10 - 10
E-Mail	sales@m-m-sports.com
E-Books	www.m-m-sports.com

All books available as E-books.

MEYER
& MEYER
SPORT

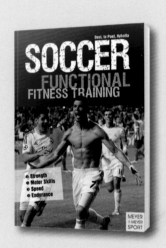

Dost I te Poel I Hyballa

SOCCER FUNCTIONAL FITNESS TRAINING

Strength | Motor Skills | Speed | Endurance

Cristiano Ronaldo, Zlatan Ibrahimovic, and Bastian Schweinsteiger, some of the world's best soccer players, are incredibly fit, fast, lean, and strong. Achieving this level of athleticism requires a rigorous soccer fitness training.

In *Soccer Functional Fitness Training*, the authors present numerous drills for this training. Based on latest findings in sports science and on the authors' long-term coaching experience, they present an extensive practical guide to help you improve your team's performance.

The exercises can be used for amateurs and professional players, youth and adults alike. Your players can learn how to score the most exciting and acrobatic goals, how to tackle without fouling, and how to avoid injuries.

448 p., in color,
573 photos, 83 illustrations,
57 charts, paperback
6 1/2" x 9 1/4"

ISBN: 9781782550907

$ 34.95 US/$ 51.95 AUS
£ 23.95 UK/€32.95

MEYER & MEYER Sport
Von-Coels-Str. 390
52080 Aachen
Germany

Phone	+49 02 41 - 9 58 10 - 13
Fax	+49 02 41 - 9 58 10 - 10
E-Mail	sales@m-m-sports.com
E-Books	www.m-m-sports.com

All books available as E-books.

MEYER & MEYER SPORT